The Stansberry Research

GUIDE TO
INVESTMENT
BASICS

By Ken Little

Published by Stansberry Research

Edited by Fawn Gwynallen

About Stansberry Research

Founded in 1999 and based out of Baltimore, Maryland, Stansberry Research is the largest independent source of financial insight in the world. It delivers unbiased investment advice to self-directed investors seeking an edge in a wide variety of sectors and market conditions.

Stansberry Research has nearly two dozen analysts and researchers – including former hedge-fund managers and buy-side financial experts. They produce a steady stream of timely research on value investing, income generation, resources, biotech, financials, short-selling, macro-economic analysis, options trading, and more.

The company's unrelenting and uncompromised insight has made it one of the most respected and sought-after research organizations in the financial sector. It has nearly one million readers and more than 500,000 paid subscribers in over 100 countries.

About the Author

"I believe anyone can learn to be a successful investor. Simply learn the basics and be open to unbiased expert advice." – Ken Little

Ken Little started writing about investing – online and in print – in 1997.

He is the author of 15 books that explain the basics of investing and personal finance, including *The Complete Idiot's Guide to Stock Investing* and *Teach Yourself Investing in 24 Easy Lessons*. He is the technical editor of two others.

And he has written more than 650 articles for the Stocks page on About.com.

Previously, Ken was the online writer for Strong Mutual Funds (now part of Wells Fargo) and the vice president of marketing for major financial services company USAA. He also served as the business editor for the *San Antonio Express-News*.

Table of Contents

Introduction   i

What Is Investing?   1

Stocks   11
I   Common Shares   13
II   Preferred Shares   14
III   Stock Classifications   16
IV   Companies by Size   20
V   Stock Markets   21
VI   Stock Indexes   23
VII   Bull and Bear Markets   27
VIII   Stock Prices   28
IX   Stock Splits/Buybacks   33
X   Risk and Potential Reward in Stocks   34
XI   Where Do Stocks Come From?   36
XII   How to Buy a Stock   38
XIII   Evaluating Stocks   44
XIV   Investing Strategies   62
XV   How to Make Money Investing   66
XVI   Placing an Order   69
XVII   Exit Strategies   72

Bonds   75
XIX   Bonds and Risk   84
XX   Rating a Bond   88
XXI   Types of Bonds   90

Mutual Funds 97

XXIII   Fund Management   104

XXIV   Types of Mutual Funds   105

XXV   Mutual-Fund Strategies   107

XXVI   Management Fees   109

XXVII   Picking a Mutual Fund   110

XXVIII   Taxes   110

Exchange-Traded Funds 113

XXIX   Bond ETFs   114

XXX   Sector ETFs   114

XXXI   ETFs vs. Mutual Funds   115

XXXII   ETF Investing Strategies   118

Options, Futures, Currencies, and Others 119

XXXIII   Derivatives   120

XXXIV   So What Is an Option?   121

XXXV   Key Terms   122

XXXVI   Call Option   123

XXXVII   Put Option   124

XXXVIII   Futures Contracts   125

XXXIX   Currency Trading   129

LXXI   Key Economic Terminology   131

If You're Interested in More Knowledge 135

Glossary 137

Introduction

By Brian Hunt

Congratulations… and welcome to the *Stansberry Research Guide to Investment Basics.*

We say "congratulations" because if you're new to investing, you're taking an important first step. It's one many would-be investors never take.

Many folks rush blindly into investing. They don't learn the basics. They don't learn vital lessons that could save them years of frustration and losses. They spend more time learning about a potential new car purchase than how to invest their life savings.

Investors who refuse to learn always lose.

If you're reading this book, you're taking the first step to ensure you're not one of those people. You're making the commitment to learn and build a vital knowledge base.

And for that, you deserve a "congratulations."

We believe anyone with average intelligence and a willingness to learn can become a successful investor.

But realize: Just like any worthwhile skill, it takes work and study to become a successful investor. If you're willing to learn, follow time-tested steps, and be open to expert advice, there's no reason you can't succeed in the markets.

This guide is a great first step in getting a good investment education. It's an overview of the many elements in the world of investing. These basic pieces, when fit together, make up what will become your investing strategy.

This guide will help you understand:

- The definition and purpose of investing
- The role of risk in investing
- The components of investing
- Stocks
- Bonds
- Mutual funds and exchange-traded funds
- Exotic tools for the advanced investor (like options)
- Some basic economic concepts

The goal of every investor is to earn the highest returns while taking the least amount of risk. This guide will help you better understand the stock market and the various tools you need to reach this goal.

Stansberry Research has been helping investors with independent investment advice since 1999. We serve nearly one million readers in more than 120 countries with solid advice through our investment research newsletters. Unlike most every other financial institution, our research is unbiased and independent.

We are not paid by any company or organization to mention them favorably. In fact, more than a few have threatened us with legal action because they did not like the conclusions our analysts reached. Any company, website, or organization recommended in this guide is there because we believe it can benefit you.

Before you go further... we must issue an important warning...

This book will provide you with a solid foundation of investing basics. But if you don't know how to <u>make</u> money and <u>save</u> money, investment knowledge won't be of much use to you.

You're very, very unlikely to "get rich quick" by investing a small sum of money in the stock market. *Always remember that smart investing is about preserving and growing wealth. It's not about getting rich quick.*

Before you invest a nickel in stocks or bonds, make sure you know how to earn an income through a job or by owning your own business. Make sure you're free of destructive credit-card debt. Make sure you have enough cash on hand for at least three months of living expenses.

You should only consider investing after you've mastered making and saving money.

If you already have these two down, let's get started!

Regards,

Brian Hunt
Editor in Chief
Stansberry Research

— 1 —
What Is Investing?

We'll start this guide with a claim that might seem outrageous to you...

You don't have to take big risks to make big money in the stock market.

This claim runs counter to what many financial advisors and mainstream magazines say about investing. Many people will tell you that to make big returns, you have to take big risks.

This isn't the case at all.

It's one of the "old wives tales" of investing.

Making big investment returns DOES NOT have to involve taking big risks.

Making big returns the Stansberry Research way involves acquiring a basic knowledge of investing. It involves knowing how to value things like stocks and bonds... and making sure you never overpay for them.

It involves avoiding investments that are popular and expensive... and flocking toward investments that are unloved and trading for bargain prices.

When you learn the basics of stocks and bonds – and the tools you need to accurately value them – you'll see it's not complicated at all.

Which investing methods you use depend on many factors, such as risk tolerance, age, and investment goals. But as we said, investing in the markets won't do you any good unless you already know how to save. Despite what you may believe, the two concepts are not the same.

Saving

Investing is not the same as saving. **Saving** is a passive form of money management. **Investing** is an active way to increase your net worth.

When we use the term "saving," we refer to basic products such as:

- Savings accounts
- Bank certificates of deposit
- Short-term U.S. Treasury products (like T-bills)

Most savings products have some form of guarantee or insurance that your money will be safe. But that safety has a price: low returns (aka low interest rates).

Savings vehicles hold money for use in the near future – like a down payment on a new car. They're also good for money you need to access quickly in case of emergency.

"With saving, you sacrifice a good return for the safety of your principal. With investing, you sacrifice some of the safety of your principal for an expected higher return."

However, the low interest rates paid by these products make them ill-suited for accumulating and growing wealth. The erosive effects of inflation and taxes mean these savings products will earn even less – and sometimes you will actually lose money.

Risk

In 2013, one-year bank CDs were paying less than 1% interest. That same year, the stock market was up 29%, as measured by the S&P 500 Index.

What was the difference between those returns?

If you bought a $10,000, one-year bank CD on January 2, 2013 and cashed it in when it matured in January 2014, you'd have received $10,000 and change. You knew that is what it would be worth. Even if the bank failed, the FDIC insured your $10,000. Your money was safe for that period. You didn't lose it. But you didn't do much to increase it, either.

Say you put that money in the stock market on January 2, 2013 instead. You would have had no idea what it would be worth in 12 months. It's a riskier move than the CD. As it turned out, 2013 was a good year to be in the stock market (as measured by the S&P 500).

If you had invested $10,000, you would have ended the year with about $13,200. That's a much better return than the CD.

Of course, there was no guarantee the market would do so well. There are years when the overall stock market loses money.

That's the difference between saving and investing. With saving, you sacrifice a good return for the safety of your principal. With investing, you sacrifice some of the safety of your principal for an expected higher return.

Investing is riskier than saving, but potentially more rewarding.

Risk vs. Potential Reward

Understanding the relationship between risk and potential reward is one of the foundations of your investing education.

Too many investors don't understand this relationship. This leads them to make investment choices that carry too much risk for too little potential reward.

Your goal as an investor is to maximize your return, while minimizing your risk. Each investor will approach this differently.

What seems like a risky investment for one investor may seem reasonable to another. As your investing education proceeds, you will find the level of risk that works for you.

This guide will help you identify the risk characteristics of the basic investing tools you will use to reach your financial goals.

The Power of Compound Interest

Compounding of interest is the most powerful tool at an investor's disposal.

It is the greatest wealth-builder available to individuals and is the force behind successful, long-term investing.

The power of compounding is in the:

- Rate of return
- The initial investment
- The time the investment is held

Here are some illustrations to better understand that…

Suppose you invested $1,000 in an account that pays 7% annually. Each year, you collect $70 in interest on that $1,000. If the account had a fixed rate of return, you would receive $70 each subsequent year. At the end of 10 years, the account will have paid you $700 in interest. You still have your original $1,000 for a total of $1,700.

Now let's see what happens if you reinvest those earnings instead…

Investors unleash the real power of compounding when they reinvest their earnings. **Reinvested earnings allow investors to earn interest on their interest.**

For example, you invest $1,000 and it earns 7% a year.

The first year, you earn $70 dollars, which you reinvest.

The second year, you earn $74.90 ($1,070 x 7%), which you reinvest.

The third year, you earn $80.13 ($1,145 x 7%).

In 10 years, the value of your investment is almost $1,968. And all by reinvesting your earnings. You are $268 ahead of our example above when earnings were not reinvested.

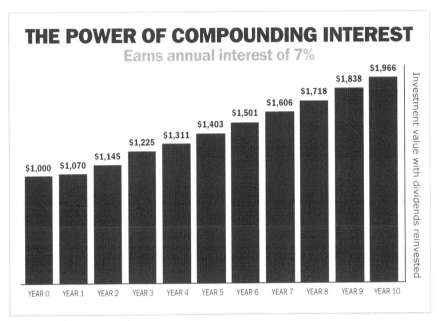

THE POWER OF COMPOUNDING INTEREST

Earns annual interest of 7%

$1,000 $1,070 $1,145 $1,225 $1,311 $1,403 $1,501 $1,606 $1,718 $1,838 $1,966

YEAR 0 YEAR 1 YEAR 2 YEAR 3 YEAR 4 YEAR 5 YEAR 6 YEAR 7 YEAR 8 YEAR 9 YEAR 10

Investment value with dividends reinvested

www.stansberryresearch.com

Now, suppose instead, you invested $1,000 in 100 shares of ABC stock at $10 per share. ABC paid a $0.70-per-share dividend. (More about dividends later.) This is about a 7% return on the $10 share price.

Also, suppose the price of the stock grew by 7% per year – a little lower than the historical average – but the dividend stayed the same. If you reinvest the dividends, that money is used to buy more shares. And those shares earn the 7% dividend also.

In 10 years, your account would more than triple to almost $3,180 and you would own about 162 shares of stock, instead of the original 100 shares. This is the power of compounding: You more than tripled your initial investment of $1,000 without investing another penny.

> *"Compound interest is the greatest wealth-builder available. It's the force behind successful, long-term investing."*

Best of all worlds: Same scenario as above except the share price increases and the dividend increases 7% per year. At the end of 10 years, your $1,000 investment is now worth $3,870.

The table on the next page compares the results of all three strategies. You can see how your dollar return increases dramatically depending on the rate of return and the share-price and dividend growth...

Value of $1,000 at 7% after 10 Years			
Simple Interest	Reinvested Interest	Reinvested Interest w/ Share Price Growth	Reinvested Interest w/ Share Price and Dividend Growth
$1,700	$1,968	$3,180	$3,870
	+ $268	+$1,480	+$2,170

Compound interest is a tremendous wealth-building machine. You can tap into this power by picking great companies that pay great dividends and holding your investment for a long period.

To press the point, if you held the stock for 25 years (with 7% annual growth in the share price and 7% annual growth in the dividend), your initial investment of $1,000 (100 shares at $10 per share) will be worth almost $30,000.

The math here is a little complicated. You can use an online calculator, like the one on Buyupside.com. Look for the dividend-reinvestment calculator.

This is the power of compound interest and how you can use it to build your wealth. Of course, no stock will have 25 straight years of 7% growth in price and dividend. But you get the picture. **Investing is about putting the power of compound interest to work for you**.

There are other ways to make money in the stock market besides long-term investing. Almost every investor will want these alternatives to supplement the main strategy of long-term investing in great companies.

Investing vs. Trading

Investors buy stocks based on the value of the business. Investors want companies that will grow over a long period.

Traders buy and sell stocks on short-term swings in prices. Trading is more risky and more difficult than investing.

High-frequency traders are also known as **day traders**. They make or lose money by small swings in price. They typically trade a large number of shares, so a few pennies of profit (or loss) on each trade adds up to real money.

"Successful trading requires a large amount of time and money."

Very sophisticated computer programs may perform the actual trades, buying and selling tens of thousands of shares in seconds – much faster than a human.

The stock market is chaotic over short periods. Many complex factors push prices up or down. It's not for beginners. It's best to only consider trading short-term movements after you have at least five years of successful investing under your belt.

— 2 —
Stocks

Counter to what many people think, a "stock" isn't some piece of paper meant for trading for a few weeks. And it's not a lottery ticket.

When you buy a stock, you are buying partial ownership of a business.

If you get nothing else from this book, please get this concept. Many people never understand it, and it leads to huge losses over their investment careers.

It's so important, it's worth repeating...

> *"When you buy a stock, you are buying partial ownership of a business."*

Sometimes that business might be a decades-old company that reliably pays dividends, like Coca-Cola or Johnson & Johnson. Sometimes the business might be a bank. Sometimes it might be a small start-up.

Whatever the business, when you buy a stock, you become a part owner of that business.

That's why to succeed in stocks over the long run, you need

to know some key aspects of business. You need to know the basics of valuing a business. You need to know how they create value (or plan to create value) for customers and clients.

In this chapter, you'll learn the basics of stocks... and the terms used when talking about them...

———————•———————

When you buy a "share" of stock, you are a part owner of the company.

As a part owner of a company, you have rights. You can vote on certain matters of importance to the company, most often by mail. Owners – also known as "shareholders" or "stockholders" – elect the board of directors. The board of directors watches out for the interests of all owners.

Shareholders profit if the company is successful. The price of the stock they own rises, and they can sell their shares for a profit.

You also have certain risks. If the company is not successful, the value of your shares declines.

There are two broad types of stock shares: common and preferred. In most cases, when people talk about stocks, they mean common shares.

Common Shares

Common shares are traded on the stock markets. They're the shares referred to when news sources report "stocks were up (or down) today."

In most cases, you will have one vote for each share you own. However, this may not be correct for every stock. For example, a company can issue (sell) different classes of stock.

The founders of a company may want to control the board of directors. They create a class of stock that has 10 votes for every share (Google, for example). Before buying a stock, find out if there are special classes and what that means to you.

Small investors – people who own less than 5% of a stock, for example – have little influence on the board of directors.

Dividends

Some common stocks pay dividends. A **dividend** is a payment of profits to the owners. The board of directors sets the dividend rate annually.

The board of directors can change or drop the dividend. The company does not have to pay owners of common shares a dividend. Most dividends are paid quarterly, but the rate is quoted annually.

If you own 100 shares of common stock that pays a $2 annual dividend, you will receive $200 per year in four checks for $50 each.

A dividend reinvestment plan (or "DRIP") lets you buy more shares of stock. Reinvesting your dividends is a great way to build wealth. Remember our example of compounding interest.

"A dividend is a payment of profits to the owners of a stock."

Some companies, especially younger ones, choose not to pay a dividend. Profits are used to finance growth. Investors buy "growth" companies for the rate at which the stock price climbs.

Other companies pay a regular dividend that may increase over time. Investors are attracted to "income" stocks for the dividend and any rise in the stock's price. An income stock's price may not rise as fast as a growth stock.

Preferred Shares

Preferred shares are the other type of stock a company can issue. Preferred shares pay a stated dividend. The company must pay this dividend first. Only then can it pay common-share dividends.

Investors who want current income may be attracted to preferred shares. Some retirees use preferred stock to provide income for daily expenses.

Companies sell preferred shares to raise money that does not have to be paid back. Only companies with a solid, mature business issue preferred stock.

Preferred shares have no voting rights in company business.

If the company goes broke, preferred shares may get cash if any money is left after all debts are paid.

Regulation

The **Securities and Exchange Commission (SEC)** regulates the stock market. It requires all companies to report anything that may affect the stock's price – so all investors have access to the same, detailed information. This information includes:

- All financial data
- Any new products, mergers, and so on
- Lawsuits or rule violations
- Changes in key leaders
- Much more

The purpose of rules is to keep companies honest with investors…

Companies must report this information every fiscal quarter. Some news – such as changes in key executives, major lawsuits, and so on – must be reported immediately.

And at year-end, the company reports financial results for the past year.

The annual report is usually a glossy magazine with lots of pictures of happy workers and customers.

It also includes detailed financial reports and other important matters. Bad news is often found deep in the text or footnotes. It is there, but usually harder to find than the good news.

You can read the same reports on the SEC website (www.sec. gov) without the photos. The annual report is the 10-K and the quarterly report is the 10-Q.

Companies must follow SEC rules – which include reporting deadlines and detailed financial disclosures – to sell stock to the public.

Stock Classifications

Investors classify stocks in many different ways. These include:

Blue-Chip (Core) Stock

A **blue-chip (or core) stock** is considered one of the safest to buy. Very stable, mature businesses may have blue-chip stocks. The blue-chip label refers to the most expensive chip in a poker game.

Blue-chip stocks are not the most expensive. However, they do represent a "safe" haven. Blue-chip stocks may not have as big increases or decreases in price as other stocks during big market moves.

Growth Stock

A **growth stock** grows rapidly in price as the company grows. Investors who buy at the right price can see quick profits.

However, as the company's growth slows over time, the stock's growth also slows. When growth slows, investors often sell… causing a rapid drop in price. Investors must know when to buy and when to sell to profit.

Value Stock

The market price of a **value stock** is less than its true value. Value investors buy the stock at this low price and hold it. There are many reasons the stock is priced too low.

When the market re-prices the stock to its true value, the investor profits. Many successful investors made their fortunes with value stocks.

It is important to know the value and price are not the same. **Value** is what a company is worth as an ongoing business. **Price** is what the stock trades for at any point in time. That price may or may not have anything to do with the value of the company.

Income Stock

An **income stock** pays a consistent and growing dividend. Investors profit from the dividends and any price growth. Dividends can be re-invested. Utilities are often good income stocks. They may not grow much, but they provide steady dividend payments.

Stock Sectors

Stock sectors are groupings of common industry types. Sectors help investors compare the stocks of like companies. Here's a basic list of different sectors:

- Basic Materials
- Capital Goods
- Communications
- Consumer staples
- Energy
- Financial
- Health Care
- Technology
- Utilities

You can find a similar list at biz.yahoo.com/p/. Here you can see a comparison with the other sectors. Each of these sectors breaks down into much more detail. You can compare stocks in the same detailed grouping.

Cyclical and Non-Cyclical Stocks

Cyclical and non-cyclical stocks describe how they react to economic changes. **Cyclical stocks** tend to move with the economy. If the economy is growing, cyclical stocks grow as well. But a slowing economy may slow their growth also.

Non-cyclical stocks do not react as much to economic moves. Consumer staples and utilities are non-cyclical stocks. Think of it this way: You always need toilet paper and electricity. Investors often move money into these sectors when the economy goes south.

American Depositary Receipts (ADRs)

American Depositary Receipts are a way to buy shares of some foreign companies. They represent shares of foreign stock. But they are traded in U.S. dollars rather than the native currency. ADRs are traded on major stock exchanges.

Real Estate Investment Trusts (REITs)

Real Estate Investment Trusts are a special security traded on major stock exchanges. They invest in real estate projects either directly or by buying mortgages. REITs are a way to own real estate with the ability to buy and sell as easily as trading stocks.

Companies by Size

Size is another way to group stocks for comparison. Many investors favor the stock of larger companies. They see those stocks as safer and more stable. Stocks of smaller companies may be seen as more risky.

You can measure a company's size many ways. Investors use market capitalization as a common measurement. **Market cap** measures the total market value of the company's stock. It helps you target certain companies by size and gives you a basis for comparing. It also helps you understand one part of the risk picture for a company.

Here is the formula…

$$MARKET\ CAP = OUTSTANDING\ SHARES \times PRICE\ OF\ ONE\ SHARE$$

Market cap answers the question: What would it cost to buy every share of a company's stock? For example, if a company has 100 million shares outstanding and the per-share price is $15, the market cap would be $1.5 billion.

Investors group stocks into various categories based on market cap. Here is an example:

- Micro cap – less than $300 million
- Small cap – $300 million to $2 billion
- Mid cap – $2 billion to $10 billion
- Large cap – $10 billion to $200 billion
- Mega cap – more than $200 billion

There is no agreement about these numbers. You may see other market-cap scales. The important thing is to understand which classification of stock you're buying.

In general, larger-cap stocks are less volatile and risky than smaller ones. Larger companies may suffer less in economic or market downturns. They may also not rise as quickly or as far in an upswing.

Smaller companies are at more risk in a downturn but may rise quickly in an upturn. And they often lack the resources to protect market share. Smaller companies can be hurt when larger competitors go after their customers.

Stock Markets

Stock markets bring buyers and sellers together. The markets or exchanges and your broker take care of all the paper work for a small fee.

Thanks to mergers, there are two major stock exchanges remaining. The constitution for the **New York Stock Exchange (NYSE)** was drafted in 1817. And it still maintains a trading floor. The NYSE is home to the oldest and most prestigious companies in America.

Stocks that trade on the NYSE include well-known companies like La-Z-Boy Incorporated (LZB), Abercrombie & Fitch (ANF), and The Walt Disney Company (DIS).

The **Nasdaq** was the first large all-electronic exchange. Today, computer networks make most trades on all exchanges. The Nasdaq grew as the home of the technology industry. Many giants of technology began as small companies listed on the Nasdaq.

There are other smaller and special-purpose exchanges. But they just supplement the two major exchanges.

Stocks that trade on the Nasdaq include big companies like Microsoft (MSFT), Amazon (AMZN), and Costco (COST).

Electronic Communication Networks (ECN) offer another way of buying and selling stocks. ECNs connect buyers and sellers directly without going through an exchange. Large investors such as insurance companies, mutual funds, and pension funds may be clients.

There are other smaller markets that trade in stocks not eligible for listing on any major exchange. **Over the Counter (OTC)** is a way to trade stocks through dealers. These companies are too small to be listed on one of the major exchanges.

These stocks may be thinly traded, like penny stocks. It is often difficult to find information about the companies because the OTC market doesn't have the same reporting requirements as stock indexes like the Nasdaq or NYSE.

Penny stocks often trade for less than $1 per share. Penny stocks may be used in scams and should be avoided by beginning investors.

Many foreign countries and economic zones have stock markets, as well. It is becoming easier to trade on these markets. Market watchers keep an eye on foreign exchanges. They can signal trouble or opportunities in local economies.

Stock Indexes

Investors need ways to measure stock market activity. An **index** tracks the activity of a selected group of stocks over time. Indexes also track bonds and many other securities.

Indexes are quoted in points, not dollars. They are also quoted in a percentage change from the previous day. Most investors focus on the percentage change. You can use the percentage change to compare a stock to the index.

For example, if you saw the index was up 68 points for the day and the stock was up $2.36, that wouldn't help you... because that doesn't give you any context. But if you saw the index was up 2.3% and the stock was up 4.8%, that would tell you something about demand for the stock.

Here's an example, comparing the performance of Big Tech company IBM with the S&P 500 index. As you can see from their percent return, IBM lagged its index from May 2013 to May 2014...

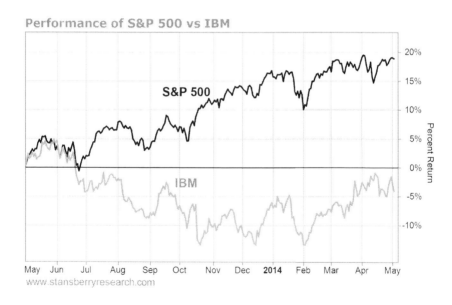

Performance of S&P 500 vs IBM

www.stansberryresearch.com

Stock indexes are complex math formulas. Some give more weight to the price of the stock. Others favor the size of the company.

The point is you can use index values many different ways. It's important to know what an index is really telling you. The way it's designed determines what you can learn from it. None of the stock indexes are simple.

The **Dow** is the oldest and most widely known stock index. The Dow Jones Industrial Average is an index of 30 stocks. These stocks seldom change. They are considered leaders in their particular industry sectors.

The Dow is price weighted. Higher-priced stocks have more influence on the index. Price is not an indicator of company size.

The Dow represents 30 of the most prestigious companies. But it ignores mid- and small-sized companies and is not a good representation of the broad stock market. These flaws are outweighed by the popularity of the index and its emotional significance.

Despite its flaws, the Dow represents about 25% of the total market's value. It reflects the immediate mood of the stock market. However, most investors do not use the Dow to represent the stock market. Its narrow focus on 30 large companies doesn't represent the thousands of other stocks being traded.

Stocks traded in the Dow include 3M (MMM), Intel (INTC), Johnson & Johnson (JNJ), and McDonald's (MCD).

The **S&P 500 Index** measures 500 of the largest corporations. It's the most widely used proxy of the market. However, it is biased toward large companies. It is calculated using market cap. This means the price changes of larger-cap stocks have a greater influence on the index.

Many consider the S&P 500 to be a more accurate reflection of the health of large corporations than the Dow. It represents a broader selection of companies in size and industry. There are more than 5,000 stocks traded on the Nasdaq and the NYSE.

Stocks in the S&P 500 include household names like Johnson & Johnson (JNJ), JPMorgan Chase (JPM), and Wal-Mart (WMT).

The **Nasdaq Composite Index** covers the almost 3,000 stocks and other securities traded there. It is market-cap weighted, which gives larger-cap companies more influence.

This index gives a good picture of the relative health of a broad selection of companies. Because there is a wide disparity in the size and age of Nasdaq stocks, the index is not as widely regarded.

Stocks traded on the Nasdaq include Apple (AAPL), eBay (EBAY), Cisco (CSCO), and Google (GOOG).

The Dow, S&P 500, and Nasdaq are the best-known and most-quoted indexes in the world. However, there are hundreds of other indexes covering just about every type of security. These indexes are useful to investors if used correctly.

You can compare a stock's performance to its index. For example, did a large-cap stock perform as well as or better than the S&P 500 Index?

During trading hours, indexes are updated in real time. But the quotes you see on most free websites are delayed up to 20 minutes. The quote you see is not the most current. That's generally OK for investors. But traders must have real-time information.

Bull and Bear Markets

Bull and bear markets refer to whether there are more buyers or sellers in the market for a long period. During daily trading, the balance between buyers and sellers will often shift several times.

The origin of the terms "bull" and "bear" is unclear. "Bull" may come from the way a bull attacks – horns down, then thrust upward. Bears slash with a downward motion, which describes stock prices in a bear market.

When there is a strong interest in stocks that pushes prices higher, it is a **bull market**. A climb of 20% or more over a two-month period is one definition. During long bull markets, investors are confident about the economy and the stock market. The major indexes show an upward trend over time.

A **bear market** happens when people dump their stocks over an extended period of time. Some define a bear market as a decline of 20% or more over a two-month period. Investors are nervous about the future of the economy. Stock indexes fall. In a bear market, investors may sell and not reinvest the proceeds.

Stock Prices

The **stock price** you see in a stock quote isn't "set" by anyone or the exchange. It's simply the amount a buyer and seller agree on at that moment. The price may change for the next trade.

Every time a share of stock is traded, the price may change. During trading hours, prices may change by the second or faster. Most of the time, those changes are a penny up or down.

Supply and demand ultimately decide stock prices. External factors – like economic, political, or global news – only push traders toward buying or selling.

When there are more sellers in the market than buyers, prices fall. Sellers must lower prices to attract buyers.

When there are more buyers in the market than sellers, prices rise. Buyers must raise their offer to attract sellers.

If there is significant news about a company after trading hours, its opening stock price may be adjusted. But after the market opens, supply and demand take over.

"Remember: Stock price and stock value are not the same thing."

As noted above, stock quotes provide many different prices besides the current one. These prices help you understand quotes and some of the stock market jargon.

Opening price: The opening price is what the stock begins trading for that day. In most cases, it is the same as the previous day's closing price. Some days, adjustments are made as noted above.

Closing price: The closing price is the final price of a stock when trading closes for the day. It may be adjusted slightly to correct for delayed trades.

Market price: The market price is the price of the stock at the most recent trade of the day. It will change constantly during trading days. It shows up as the current price on services like Yahoo Finance and Google Finance.

Bid and ask price: The price you pay for a stock is not the market price. That was the last trade. There are two prices to every trade. The **bid price** is what a buyer is willing to pay. The **ask price** is what the seller will take. The difference is called the spread. The spread goes to the exchange or market manager.

You pay the ask price if you are a buyer. You receive the bid price if you are a seller.

Stock prices are quoted in dollars and cents, not points like indexes. So in this sample screen shot from Yahoo Finance below, Apple trades for $100.02 per share...

Apple Inc. (AAPL) - NasdaqGS ⭐ Watchlist

100.02 ⬆0.21(0.21%) 11:32AM EDT - Nasdaq Real Time Price

Prev Close:	99.81	Day's Range:	98.89 - 100.52
Open:	100.34	52wk Range:	69.91 - 103.74
Bid:	100.35 x 2900	Volume:	25,334,176
Ask:	100.36 x 3000	Avg Vol (3m):	56,211,400

All publicly traded companies have a **stock symbol** for reporting purposes. These abbreviations make it easier to compress more data into small spaces on your computer screen.

On the NYSE, "F" stands for Ford. "GE" stands for General Electric. "ALL" stands for Allstate.

Many stocks on the Nasdaq have symbols with four letters. "AAPL" is Apple. "CSCO" is Cisco. However, Facebook is "FB."

To look up a price quote, it's helpful to know the symbol of the stock. But most finance websites also have a "type ahead" feature, which makes it easy to find a stock by starting to type in its full name.

A **stock quote** is the price the security is trading for at any time during the day. When the market is open, the information is updated in real time. If you have access to real-time data, the quote will constantly change. Most websites that provide this information also include many other pieces of information.

Understanding Stock Quotes ↵

The amount of data in stock quotes varies from source to source. However, most report the following information followed by an example:

Name and symbol: Apple (AAPL)

Current price: Change from previous price or close and percentage change.

Previous close: The last trade or close from the previous day.

Open: What the stock opened at.

Bid: Best price a buyer is willing to pay. Sometimes a number follows this price with an "x" in front of it. That is the number of shares the bidder is willing to buy at that price.

Ask: Best price a seller will accept. May include number of shares seller has at this price.

Day's range: The high and low for that trading day.

52-week range: The high and low for the previous 52 weeks.

Volume: Number of shares traded, sometimes reported in millions.

Average volume: Number of shares traded on an average day.

Some websites include this information on graphs and charts, which can be easier to read.

The quotes usually include much more information. We'll look at the other quote data and more in later sections.

Online or Print Quotes

It's important to have access to the most up-to-date stock-price information – especially for traders. You can get current information through your stockbroker or paid services. (Again, quotes from websites like Yahoo Finance and Google Finance tend to be delayed.)

A few newspapers still print stock-market information. Business newspapers and some local newspapers carry stock tables. You obviously get delayed information in a newspaper.

It is your choice. But for the most up-to-date information, you can't beat websites.

Stock Splits/Buybacks

Stock splits and buybacks may affect a stock's price, but for different reasons. Stock splits happen when a company divides the existing shares. Stock buybacks occur when a company buys shares of its own stock.

A **stock split** happens when the company splits its existing shares into more shares. A company with 50 million shares outstanding could split those 2-for-1. Every share of existing stock becomes two shares. The result of a 2-for-1 split is there are now 100 million shares. The market reduces the price of the stock by half.

Why would a company do this? If the share price was very high, a split would lower the price. This makes it easier to buy standard 100-share lots. Before the split, 100 shares would cost $10,000. After the split, 100 shares cost $5,000.

There is some evidence that a lower price per share attracts investors.

Also more shares in the market may mean it is easier to find buyers and sellers.

There is also a **reverse split**, which has the opposite effect. If a company does a 1-for-2 split, it reduces the number of shares outstanding. This doubles the stock's price.

A **stock buyback** is when the company buys its own shares. A company may buy back its own shares to increase per-share price. A reduced supply of shares creates higher demand for the remaining shares.

A buyback may offer shareholders the option to sell shares back to the company, often for more then the existing market price. The company can also buy its own shares on the open market.

Risk and Potential Reward in Stocks

The relationship between risk and potential reward is basic to understanding investing. Investing is risky – riskier than saving. You can control some of the risk. You can guard against other risks. But there will always be some element of risk involved.

Investors face two types of risk – those inside the market and those outside. How much risk you tolerate is a personal de-cision. Younger investors can take more risk. Bad results can be erased over time with less risky moves. Older investors cannot afford big risks. If they fail, there may not be enough time to recover.

Certain stocks or other types of investments are more risky than others. Investors can choose to accept the risks or not by picking more or less risky stocks.

For example, a stable, mature company like Johnson & Johnson (JNJ) is considered less risky than Netflix (NFLX). Johnson & Johnson is a huge, diversified company that pays regular dividends. Netflix is a new technology company that's always at risk of a better technology replacing it.

You can't avoid risk as an investor. But you can decide how much risk is right for you. That level of risk will change over time.

So what kinds of risks are there?

Some types of risk could affect the whole market and economy. These are beyond our control. The financial markets could collapse and the markets dive. Not much we can do to prevent an economic disaster.

When investors pour money into one sector, they can create a **bubble**. Bubbles happen when investors become over-confident. Often, certain sectors of the market will experience a bubble. Tech stocks, real estate, and other sectors have experienced bubbles.

Sometimes, the whole market is inflated. As prices rise, other investors join the rush. At some point, all bubbles burst and prices come crashing down.

How to Protect Yourself

We can't prevent bubbles or other problems in the market. But we can protect ourselves to some extent. **Diversification** is one way to provide some protection. It means don't put all your eggs in one basket. Don't invest all or even most of your money in a single stock or in the same sector.

A good rule for diversification is to begin with **no more than 5% of your capital in any one stock** and **no more than 15% in any one sector**.

Where Do Stocks Come From?

Before a company can sell its stock to the public (or "go public"), it must get permission from the SEC. It must provide complete financial information, such as revenue and profit results. It also gathers any other information investors may need to make a decision, such as biographies of the top officers, any pending lawsuits, and so on.

The complete package is called a **prospectus**. Prior to a public sale of stock, the prospectus is made available to any potential shareholders. An investment bank will help the company with the sale. A price is set for the first sale.

The first public sale of a stock is called an **initial public offering (IPO)**. IPOs are often met with excitement in the market. Some investors hope to buy the stock early in the first day.

But it's almost impossible for small investors to buy at the initial price. By the time they have a shot at buying shares, the price may have gone up substantially. Often once the excitement dies down, the stock's price falls again…

The Facebook IPO in May 2012 was highly anticipated. The stock opened at $38 per share. By September, it was down to $18.50 per share. Shares did not return to the initial price of $38 until August 2013.

An IPO is the only time a company sells stock directly to the public in most cases (unless the company releases new shares). Once shares are in the public market, trading occurs between buyers and sellers. The company does not receive any money from those sales.

When you buy 100 shares of stock, it's from another investor. When you sell 100 shares of stock, you receive the money.

How to Buy a Stock

Buying a stock begins with a three-step process…

1. Select a stockbroker and open an account.
2. Identify a stock that meets your investing goals (more on this later).
3. Purchase the stock.

Learning how to identify which stock is a good investment for you can be a complex process. So we'll get to that in a few pages. First, we'll show you how to pick a stockbroker, what types of investment accounts you can open, how to place an order to buy or sell a stock, and two important exit strategies to keep in mind…

Role of the Stockbroker

In every stock trade, there are two major parties – the buyer and the seller. To help the buyer and the seller make trades, there's a stockbroker, a market manager, and/or an exchange (like the NYSE or Nasdaq).

The role of the stockbroker in a simple trade is to enter the details into a computer connected to the exchange. If you are buying, the broker would enter an order to buy, say, 100 shares of Dell at $24 per share. If you are selling, the order would be to sell 100 shares at $24.

In this simple example, the exchange matches the orders and the trade happens. The buyer and seller pay their brokers a fee.

Large investors can shortcut this process. But most of us need a stockbroker to enter orders and process the details.

The role of the stockbroker is to facilitate trades. Depending on the type of broker, they may take on additional responsibilities, such as providing advice or research. The more assistance they provide, the higher their fees.

Here are four broad categories of brokers to give you an idea of what is available…

1. Discount/online broker
2. Discount broker-with-assistance
3. Full service broker
4. Money manager

The traditional **discount/online broker** is an order taker. It will take your order either over the phone or online.

If it is over the phone, you will speak to a live stockbroker. But unless you stumble over the technical aspects of an order, discount/online brokers will leave all the decisions about your investment account up to you. They won't help you pick a stock or tell you when to sell.

On the other hand, if you are dealing with a discount broker online, you may never actually talk to a human. You just enter your order online, and it gets filled.

Some online brokers offer access to research. They may have account management tools online or that you can download.

Discount/online-with-assistance brokers will offer some help to customers... But they do not offer full-service consulting. Their sites typically have more research than a traditional discount brokerage does. It may offer newsletters with investing tips (but not necessarily stock recommendations).

The traditional **full-service broker** provides recommendations for specific stocks. The broker does a financial assessment to determine your needs and suitability for various investments.

The broker puts together an investing plan that you review and adjust periodically. This service is great if you don't have the time or inclination to make your own investment decisions. However, you will pay extra for the service in trading fees.

A **money manager** – also known by several other names – handles large portfolios, which means you should have a hefty sum to invest before considering this route.

Money managers take responsibility for investing decisions in exchange for a percentage of the assets they manage. This is expensive. But a good money manager is worth his weight in gold.

So which kind of broker is right for you?

There are many brokers that may not fit neatly in one of the above groups. The lines aren't always clear. Many investors want little or no help and choose the lowest-cost broker (discount/online). Other investors want more help making decisions. There is no correct answer. You must decide what you need and what you are willing to pay.

Below, is a table that compiles the most important information about these kinds of brokers. Study it, and decide which type best suits your needs…

	Online/discount broker	Full service broker
Simple trade	$6-$15 average commission	Up to $150 per trade
Advice	Not typically	Yes. Investment suggestions
Annual fee	Not typically	Around $150 per year
Free trades	No	With annual fee on assets of 1% to 1.5% with minimum often in six figures.
Trade online	Yes	Not typically
Trade by phone	Yes	Yes

Types of Investment Accounts

There are several types of accounts that most brokers offer. Here are the three most common:

1. Cash account
2. Margin account
3. Discretionary account

A **cash account** is the simplest type of brokerage account and the first one you will open.

Online and discount brokers require a minimum deposit before they will open your account. Many offer an interest-bearing account until you are ready to trade.

When you sell a stock, the broker will deposit the proceeds in the account (unless you instruct them otherwise), so cash is available for the next purchase.

Margin accounts allow you to borrow up to 50% of the value of the stock from your broker. For example, say you want to buy $10,000 of stock at $100 per share. With a margin account, you put up $5,000 and borrow $5,000 from your broker.

By borrowing one-half the value of the stock, you can multiply your profits dramatically. Here's how that works: If the price of the stock doubles to $20,000, your investment triples. You repay the $5,000 to the broker (plus interest) and the remaining $15,000 is yours.

However, there is risk. Leverage – the use of borrowed money to increase your return – works both ways.

For example, you borrow $5,000 to buy $10,000 in stock at $100 per share. The stock falls to $50 per share. The position is now worth $5,000.

When the stock falls to a price preset by the broker, he will issue a "margin call."

"Margin can be a powerful tool, but it can also be risky. Beginning investors should avoid margin accounts."

When you get a margin call, you have two options. You can deposit cash into the account to raise the value to the broker's limit. Or you can sell the stock immediately and pay off the loan. Some brokers may not give you the option of depositing cash. They may sell for you when the stock falls below a certain price.

If the broker sells at $50 per share, the $5,000 pays off the loan and you are out your $5,000 investment, plus interest to the broker. (This example ignores fees, interest, and other factors.)

Discretionary accounts give a broker the right to buy and sell stock without notifying you. *Unless you trust a broker completely, never give anyone this type of control over your finances.* It is the equivalent of a blank check.

Evaluating Stocks

One of the most important topics we'll cover in this section is how to pick the right stock for you...

Identifying stocks for investment is an investor's most important job. Investing on instinct or "going with your gut" is a recipe for disaster. You need a strategy for identifying and qualifying good stocks.

Investors buy companies, not stocks. Your investigation begins with identifying quality companies – like companies that pay good and growing dividends.

There are many helpful websites that offer opinions on stocks. Some are free. Others cost money. Be open to taking advantage of the expert advice available online. However, be very cautious about who you trust for help...

There are many honest stockbrokers who will help you decide which stocks are right for you. They can be a source of advice. But remember they get paid every time you buy or sell. It is wise to consider advice from experts who do not profit when you buy or sell.

Whether you make your own decisions or consider advice from experts – we recommend you do both – you need to have a basic understanding of how companies are evaluated. Investing is all about numbers, but you don't have to be a math whiz. The important numbers are readily available from many different websites.

"Investors buy companies, not stocks."

You do, however, need a basic understanding of where the numbers come from and what they mean. This will help you verify a company's value.

Remember: Price and value are not the same.

This is one of the basic concepts that new investors must grasp. The quote that captures this idea best is by legendary investor Ben Graham: "Price is what you pay. Value is what you get."

Your job is to identify the value in companies and determine what they're really worth... not what the market says, but the real value. When the price drops below that value, the company becomes an investment candidate.

Here's how you determine a company's value...

Earnings

Earnings are the profit a company creates. *It is the single most important number when evaluating a company.*

You need to know...

1. How much money is the company making?
2. How much is it going to make in the future?

Dividends and rising stock prices – which create wealth for shareholders – come from earnings or anticipated earnings.

When earnings fall short, the stock price often falls. Companies report earnings every quarter. If they fall short of projected earnings, major analysts immediately sound the alarm.

Earnings are found on the company's income statement. Most online services such as Yahoo Finance are a quick source for finding the latest and historical earnings. Earnings expectations differ from industry to industry. For example, investors expect higher earnings from tech companies than from companies that make staples such as toilet paper.

The best way to judge earnings (or any other financial number or ratio) is to compare two companies in the same industry. You can also compare a company's earnings to the average for the industry. Yahoo makes this easy. You can look at basic industries or drill down into comparisons of companies in sub-categories.

Earnings are important. But by themselves, they don't tell you how the market values the stock. You need to use some valuation ratios to find that out. These are easy to calculate. You can also find them on many websites, including Morningstar.com and Yahoo Finance.

Important notes about valuation ratios:

1. Never invest on the basis of one number.
2. Ratios are best used to compare companies in the same industry.
3. All have some flaws that may distort results.
4. You don't have to memorize the ratios, just know the intent.
5. These ratios and others are easily available online.

Below are some common valuation ratios...

Earnings per Share (EPS) 📎

Earnings per share (EPS) measures a company's profitability. EPS is also important in determining a reasonable share price. The formula is...

EARNINGS PER SHARE =
NET EARNINGS / OUTSTANDING SHARES

For example, if a company had net earnings of $2 billion and 200 million outstanding shares, the EPS would be $10 ($2 billion / 200 million = 10).

You use the EPS to compare two companies in the same industry. *If one has a higher EPS, you can assume it is more profitable.*

There are three types of EPS numbers. You can use these to calculate and project a company's past and future value…

Trailing EPS – last year's numbers and the only actual EPS.

Current EPS – this year's numbers, which are still projections.

Forward EPS – future numbers, which are obviously projections.

Price-to-Earnings (P/E) Ratio

The **price-to-earnings (P/E) ratio** looks at the relationship between the stock's price and the company's earnings. The P/E is the most popular metric of stock analysis, although not the only one you should consider.

The formula is…

PRICE-TO-EARNINGS RATIO =
STOCK PRICE / EARNINGS PER SHARE

For example, a company with a share price of $40 and an EPS of $4 would have a P/E of 10 ($40 / $4 = 10).

What does P/E tell you? The P/E gives you an idea of what the market is willing to pay for the company's earnings. The higher the P/E, the more the market is willing to pay. A high P/E may show an overpriced stock. It can also indicate the market has high hopes for this stock's future.

A low P/E may be a "vote of no confidence" by the market. It could also mean the market has overlooked this stock. Many investors have made their fortunes spotting these value stocks before the rest of the market discovered their true worth.

What's the "right" P/E? Part of the answer depends on your willingness to pay for earnings. The more you're willing to pay, the higher the "right" P/E is for that particular stock. Another investor may not see the same value… and think your "right" P/E is wrong.

P/E is best used when comparing stocks in the same industry. You can also compare a company's P/E to that of its sector. Like all valuation ratios, it's just one piece of the picture.

Price-to-Earnings-Growth (PEG) Ratio

The **price-to-earnings-growth (PEG) ratio** helps you look at future earnings growth. It helps forecast how your investment will perform in the future. If the company continues to grow earnings, your investment will likely increase in value.

The PEG factors in projected earnings growth rates to the P/E. This is the formula…

PRICE-TO-EARNINGS GROWTH =
PRICE TO EARNINGS / PROJECTED GROWTH IN EARNINGS

For example, a stock that has a P/E of 30 and is projected to grow its earnings at 15% next year would have a PEG of 2 (30/15 = 2).

What does the "2" mean? The lower the number, the less you pay for each unit of future earnings growth. A stock with a high P/E and higher projected earnings growth than its peers may be a good value.

For a low-P/E stock with a projected earnings growth less than its peers, you see that what looks like a value may not work out that way. A stock with a P/E of 8 and flat earnings growth (1%) equals a PEG of 8. This could prove to be an expensive investment.

A few important things to remember about PEG:

1. It is about year-to-year earnings growth.
2. It relies on projections, which may not always be accurate.

Price-to-Sales (P/S) Ratio

Some valuation metrics don't rely on earnings. **The price-to-sales (P/S)** ratio can be used on any company – not just to compare companies within the same sector. It also provides a way to look at young companies with no earnings.

This ratio looks at the current stock price relative to the total sales per share. You calculate the P/S by dividing the market cap of the stock by the total revenues of the company.

You can also calculate the P/S by dividing the current stock price by the sales per share.

$$PRICE\text{-}TO\text{-}SALES\ RATIO =$$
$$MARKET\ CAP\ /\ REVENUES$$

$$OR$$

$$PRICE\text{-}TO\text{-}SALES\ RATIO =$$
$$STOCK\ PRICE\ /\ SALES\ PER\ SHARE$$

Much like P/E, the P/S reflects the value placed on sales by the market. The lower the P/S, the better the value.

However, this is definitely not a number you want to use in isolation. When dealing with a young company with no earnings, there are many questions to answer. The P/S supplies just one answer.

51

For example in early 2014, Apple had a P/S of 3.1. The industry average was 1.7. This tells us that investors had great confidence in Apple's ability to turn sales into profits. This alone does not mean Apple is a good or bad buy at this ratio.

Companies with a low P/S (under "1" for example) may be good buys because you're not paying a high premium for sales. However, a low P/S can also mean the company is not generating much excitement among investors.

Price-to-Book (P/B) Ratio

The **price-to-book (P/B)** ratio looks at the value the market places on the book value of the company. It tells you how much a company is worth and if that value is reflected in the stock price.

First, let's look at what book value is…

Book value is what a company owns minus what it owes. It measures a company's worth.

Here's the formula to find book value…

BOOK VALUE =
ASSETS − LIABILITIES

In other words, if you wanted to close the doors of your company, this tells you how much would be left after you settled all the outstanding obligations and sold off all the assets.

A company that is a viable growing business will always be worth more than its book value for its ability to generate earnings and growth. A company that's down and out will be worth less than its book value.

Book value appeals more to value investors who look at the relationship to the stock's price by using the P/B ratio.

The formula to find the P/B ratio is…

$$\text{PRICE-TO-BOOK RATIO} = \text{SHARE PRICE} / \text{BOOK VALUE PER SHARE}$$

Like the P/E, the lower the P/B, the better the value. Value investors use a low P/B to identify potential candidates.

Only use P/B to compare companies in the same sector.

Return on Equity (ROE)

Return on equity (ROE) is one measure of how efficiently a company uses its assets to produce earnings. Here's the formula…

RETURN ON EQUITY =
NET INCOME / SHAREHOLDER'S EQUITY
(OR ROUGHLY BOOK VALUE)

Like all the valuation metrics we've discussed in this section, compare companies in the same industry to get a better picture.

ROE is a useful measure, but it does have some flaws. For example, if a company carries a large debt, the ROE is artificially higher. Since ROE uses shareholders' equity as the divisor, the more debt a company carries, the lower the equity number will be. This means dividing by a smaller number, which produces a higher ROE.

This is a good example of why one number or ratio should not be your only consideration. You want a company with high ROE compared to its peers. You just need to look at the complete financial picture.

It is more meaningful to look at the ROE over a period of the past five years to average out any abnormal numbers.

ROE is a useful tool in identifying companies with a competitive advantage. The company that earns more than its peers with its assets is often a better investment.

Dividend Yield

The **dividend yield** tells you what a company pays out to shareholders in the form of dividends. The formula is...

$$DIVIDEND\ YIELD =$$
$$ANNUAL\ DIVIDEND\ PER\ SHARE / STOCK'S\ PRICE\ PER\ SHARE$$

For example, if a company's annual dividend is $1.50 and the stock trades at $25, the dividend yield is 6% ($1.50 / $25 = 0.06, or 6%).

More mature companies and industries pay out more than younger companies. Dividend investors look for a higher dividend yield, but that may mean more risk.

A long history of consistent dividend increases is a safer strategy. A strong history of steady or growing dividends indicates the company's concern for investors. This mindset eliminates some of the risk and can mean higher returns.

Stock Screens

Searching for good investment candidates can be time con-suming. Where do you start?

One way is to use a stock-screening service available on the Internet. Two of the best **stock screens** are Morningstar.com and Yahoo Finance. These tools allow you to set some pa-rameters and narrow the field down to only those stocks that match your "screens."

For example, you can ask the screener for companies with revenue growth in excess of 15% for the past three years. You can add size, such as a market capitalization of less than $5 billion.

This might give you some potential growth stocks to look at. Some screeners let you add other qualifiers, such as industry.

Financial Statements

Publicly-traded companies make their complete financials available to anyone. However, that doesn't mean you will learn much unless you are schooled in finance.

A detailed discussion of financial statements is a book by it-self. In these pages, we'll just give you a brief overview of the three main parts of the financial statement. Each of these sections tells us something different about the company…

1. Income statement
2. Balance sheet
3. Statement of cash flow

The **income statement** reports revenue (sales) and expenses. It tells us if the company is making a profit or not.

The revenues section reports sales of products and services. If the company has several divisions, the revenue of each may be listed.

The next section is expenses. It's broken down into several categories. Analysts look for higher costs tied to higher sales and growing profits. Higher costs combined with lower sales and profits is a red flag.

The third section is a summary of income. Income is the same as "profits." When we talk about a company's profit, we're generally talking about its "net" income from a given period.

Income results are then expressed as earnings per share.

The ideal income statement shows growth in revenues and profits from year to year with a smaller increase in expenses. That means the company is thriving. And it will be a solid investment.

The **balance sheet** details the value of what the company owns (assets) and what it owes (liabilities).

The first part of the balance sheet lists the company's **assets**. These include items such as:

1. Cash
2. Accounts receivable (money owed by customers)
3. Real estate
4. Equipment
5. Inventory

Companies in different industries often report different levels of assets. A manufacturer owns equipment and real estate. A software company may have few assets compared to a manufacturing company with factories full of equipment.

The next section of the balance sheet lists the company's **liabilities**, which are monies owed to others. These include:

1. Accounts payable (unpaid bills)
2. Unpaid taxes
3. Retirement costs
4. Dividends payable.
5. Debt

The third section is **shareholders' equity** – the liabilities subtracted from the assets. This section should show positive growth from year to year. Shareholders' equity is reported in U.S. dollars. Comparing the company to its industry peers will tell you if its growth is high or low on average. You can find these numbers on Morningstar.com or Yahoo Finance.

The **statement of cash flow** tracks cash from operating, financial, and investing operations.

It follows cash into the business and out again in the form of expenses, dividends, and other charges. The statement of cash flows helps overcome accounting adjustments to the income statement. Since it follows cash, it is a good picture of how the company manages operations.

Economic Moats

A market truth is that capital always seeks earnings. A company that is creating growing wealth for its investors will draw competitors.

The term "moat" refers to one or more big advantages a company has over its competitors.

Economic moats are barriers that help great companies continue to be great investments. They make it difficult or expensive for competitors to enter the market. So a stock with a big economic moat is safer than a company with strong competitors.

Having a strong moat is no guarantee of success. But it does make it difficult to be displaced as a market or industry leader.

Large companies like Wal-Mart and McDonald's have big economic moats. No one has more market share of the discount retail or fast-food industry.

Investors have different ideas of what a strong moat should look like. Here are some general guidelines to consider...

Lower costs are a moat if the company can still earn a profit. When combined with size, it's a hard moat to breach. Wal-Mart is the obvious example of this type of moat. The company gets price concessions from vendors that other retailers can't match.

For example, orders from Wal-Mart can be so large, vendors are willing to give it a special discount. This strategy is only successful if the company can control its other costs.

Companies that lock in customers through the cost or inconvenience of leaving have a moat of value. Often customers are locked in because it would take time to switch. If customers master one product or service, they will be reluctant to choose a competing product or service.

Microsoft is a good example of this. Everyone knows how to use Microsoft Word and Windows. It would take too much time and be too steep of a learning curve to switch to a different product.

Government regulation of certain markets – casinos, for example – creates a barrier to competitors. Patents create a moat that prevents competitors from duplicating a product. Drug companies are a good example of this type of moat. A blockbuster new drug can generate tremendous profits before generic versions are available.

The best-of-class products can be a significant economic moat. The products don't have to be the best if they are perceived to be the best or are tagged as an industry standard. Apple is an example of that. A company must constantly innovate to maintain this moat.

You shouldn't buy a stock just on the width of its economic moat. Moats have a habit of drying up if companies don't manage them. But they still go a long way when evaluating a company.

Intrinsic Value

A great company is much more valuable as an ongoing business than just its book value states. That's why we must also look at intrinsic value. **Intrinsic value** is the true value of a company as measured by variables beyond the financial statements.

Certain types of investors look for companies trading below their intrinsic values. They consider these stocks bargains. They buy and hold these stocks and wait for the market to price them at or above the intrinsic value.

Investing Strategies

Value Investing

Value investing is a strategy where investors look for stocks that the market has not correctly priced. In other words, a stock that is worth more than is reflected in the current price.

Fundamentals, such as earnings growth, dividends, cash flow, and book value are more important than market factors on the stock's price. Value investors buy and hold for the long term.

In general, value investors look for a company with…

1. A price-to-earnings (P/E) ratio in the bottom 10% of its sector.
2. A PEG of less than one, which may indicate the stock is undervalued.
3. Strong earnings growth over an extended period, such as in the top 25% of its sector.
4. A price-to-book (P/B) ratio of one or less.

There are many reasons a stock may trade below its true value. Maybe it's in a sector that's out of favor with the market. Maybe the company stumbles on earnings. Or maybe it encounters legal or regulatory problems.

The value investor looks at these issues and determines whether they're a temporary or permanent problem. If the fundamentals are strong, the stock may still be a candidate.

The keys to successful value investing are:

1. Identifying a company that is worth more than its market price.
2. Buying at a price that lets you profit when the market corrects the price.

Growth investing

Growth investing is a strategy where investors look for great companies that are growing rapidly... and have the potential to keep growing.

Growth investors may not hold a stock as long as value investors because growth eventually slows.

Here are some indicators that a stock is growing and will likely continue to do so...

1. It's growing faster than its sector average.
2. It has a strong return on equity that beats the sector average and its own-five year average.
3. It boasts strong year-to-year growth in earnings per share.

The keys to successful growth investing are...

1. Identifying a company that has potential for sustained growth.

2. Calculating how long the company can sustain growth.
3. Buying the stock before its share price gets bid up by other investors. This determines your profit potential.

Income Investing

Income investing is a strategy where investors are more interested in current income than growth. They often invest in stocks that pay strong dividends. This is also called **dividend investing**.

The company must be financially sound and mature. It is often a large company with a long history of paying dividends. The income investor counts on the dividend now and into the future. Maybe he'll use the dividends to pay living expenses in retirement.

It's possible to find a great company that pays dividends and also enjoys a rising stock price. But these are still not growth companies.

These stocks are very profitable and return much of the profits to shareholders.

Income investors look for:

1. A history of dividend growth showing dividends paid in both up and down markets.
2. A dividend that has historically grown from year to year.
3. Companies that are market or sector leaders.

The keys to successful income investing are:

1. Identifying a company that has a history of dividend growth.
2. Buying the stock at a price that has room for growth. This determines your profit potential.

Dividend Reinvestment Plan (DRIP)

One of the more effective tools an investor can use to grow wealth is a **dividend reinvestment plan (or "DRIP")**. Many companies offer this service. It involves reinvesting the stock's dividend to buy more shares.

Instead of giving you the dividend every quarter, the company puts your dividend payment into a special fund. When you have enough in the fund, the company will purchase more shares for you.

Over time, this is a great way to grow wealth. Your dividends buy more shares, which generate more dividends, and on and on.

This strategy works best with companies that have a history of paying consistent and (even better) growing dividends.

How to Make Money Investing

The secret to making money in the stock market is simple: Buy low and sell high. That's not a joke. It is the core of successfully investing in the stock market.

The challenging part is to know:

1. What to buy?
2. How much to pay?
3. When to sell?

If this part were easy, you wouldn't need this book. You wouldn't need the advice of experts with decades of investing experience. And you would be rich.

Unfortunately, that's not the case. Even professionals have trouble always answering these questions correctly.

But there are ways to get it right…

For beginning investors with average intelligence, the secret is to follow time-tested techniques and be open to unbiased expert advice.

That's it.

So let's look at a few time-tested, expert-recommended techniques to help you make a lot of money in the markets...

Take a Long-Term Perspective

For beginning investors, your first strategy is to consider investing a long-term process. Too many beginners try to "get rich quick." Most fail. Growing wealth is a process that takes time and patience.

People do make money in the stock market with short-term trading. However, most that try it without expert advice seldom succeed. Most successful traders have a long-term strategy that is less risky.

Investing for the long term lets your stocks generate wealth for you. If you have the long-term view, you are less likely to jump into and out of the market. This is almost a guaranteed way to *lose* money or *not* grow your wealth. Great companies (as we'll talk about next) work for you year after year.

Buy Great Companies

The core of a long-term strategy is buying great companies. Great companies have a strong economic moat. Many pay generous dividends. As we discussed in the income investing section, investing dividends in great companies is a proven way to build wealth.

Be patient and wait for the great company you want to own to go on sale... The stock market goes up and down. Down markets are often times to find great companies at a discount. The discount helps you lock in a profit.

Value vs. Price

Company ABC is $10 per share. Company XYZ is $50 per share. Which one is the bargain?

There's no way to tell by just the share price. As we know... *price and value are not the same.*

A great company has a high value whether its stock is at $10 per share or $50 per share. The value is in its ability to build wealth for you.

The price of the stock only matters in its relationship to the company's value. If the stock is priced below the value, you may have a good buying opportunity. If it's priced above value, it's likely overbought and you should wait for a correction to buy shares.

Dividends

A company that pays consistent and growing dividends can be a great wealth-builder. As we saw at the very beginning of this book, reinvesting dividends is a proven way to build wealth.

"Reinvesting dividends is a proven way to build wealth."

Dividends add to your return along with price growth of the stock. Strong dividend-paying stocks are core additions to your investing strategy.

Stock Prices

There are only two important stock prices. The ups and downs the stock experiences while you're holding don't matter. What matters is the price when you buy and the price when you sell.

If you buy at the correct price, you will almost be guaranteed to have a profit. It's worth a lot to get the price right. Professional advice can pay for itself.

Placing an Order

To buy or sell a stock, you must place a buy or sell order.

Most online or discount brokers won't be much help in deciding what type of order to place.

Here is a simple way buy and sell orders are processed...

Think of the exchange maintaining two lists. One list has the "ask" or "sell" orders. The other has the "bid" or "buy" orders. The lists are sorted by price. The best price to buy or to sell is the first order of each list.

For example, say the sell list's top order is 100 shares at $10 per share. The second order is 100 shares at $9.90 per share. The first order to buy at $10 per share is filled. If you want to sell 100 shares fast, you will need to put a sell order in for less than $10 per share to go to the top of the list.

If you want to buy 100 shares for $9.25 and the top order is $9.50 per share, you must offer more to go to the top of the list.

If there are more buyers than sellers, the share price rises as buyers raise the bid price.

If there are more sellers than buyers, the share price falls as sellers lower their price to attract buyers.

You can use a variety of buy or sell orders to take more control over the transaction.

Some of the orders restrict the transaction by price. Others constrain it by time…

The **market order** is the simplest and quickest way to get your order filled (or completed).

A market order instructs your broker to buy or sell the stock immediately at the current market price. Market orders go to the head of the list of pending orders. But for that privilege, you pay the highest pending ask price.

Limit orders instruct your broker to buy or sell a stock at a particular price. The purchase or sale will not happen unless you get your price.

Limit orders give you control over your entry or exit point by fixing the price, which can prevent you from overpaying for a stock.

A **good 'til canceled (GTC) order** instructs your broker to keep the order active until you cancel it or until it gets filled. Obviously, you use this order with other order types to specify a time frame for the order.

Some brokers have limits on how long they will hold a GTC order.

A **day order** is any order that is not a good 'til canceled order. If your broker does not fill your order that day, you will have to re-enter it the next day.

The **all-or-none order** states you want the entire order filled or none of the order filled. You would use this type of order for thinly traded stocks. For example, if you want to buy 300 shares of a stock at $10, you may find a seller for 100 shares.

Some investors would rather hold out for the full 300 shares or forget the trade.

You may find these orders called slightly different names by some brokers, but the concept will be the same.

Exit Strategies

In order to invest successfully, you need to put as much thought into planning your **exit strategy** as you put into the research that motivates you to buy the investment in the first place.

An exit strategy is a plan for how and when you will sell your investment. If you stick to your exit strategy, it can serve as a near-foolproof way to methodically cut your losses and let your winners ride. If you follow this rule, you have the best chance of outperforming the markets. If you don't, you could lose big.

There are two main types of exit strategies we advocate: a hard stop loss and a trailing stop loss. Stop losses are when you pick a price at which to sell your investment *no matter what*. If your stock hits these price targets, you must sell. It takes the emotion out of the sell decision.

A **hard stop loss** is a price at which you sell your investment to protect against a falling market. It's designed to minimize your losses. Say you buy Microsoft for $30 per share. You place a hard stop at $27. That means if the stock falls sharply after your purchase, you'll cap your losses at 10%. You won't be tempted to cling on, hoping the stock will turn around, only to see it plummet farther.

A **trailing stop loss** is more flexible than a hard stop. It's designed more to protect your gains than cap your losses (although it does both). When a stock's price increases, the trailing stop rises along with it.

Let's take that Microsoft example again. This time, when you bought the stock at $30 per share, you immediately set a trailing stop loss of 25% – or $22.50 per share. That means that if the stock fell from your purchase point, you'd minimize your loss to just 25%.

Instead, shares climb to $40. Unlike with a hard stop, your trailing stop follows the share price higher. Your new stop is $30 (25% below $40). Even if Microsoft shares fell 25%, you'll still be breakeven on your investment. If Microsoft continued to climb to $50 per share, your trailing stop would continue to climb, too… to $37.50. And you'd be assured a 25% gain.

Most brokers give you the option to enter your stops "into the market" using stop-loss orders or trailing-stop orders.

But keep in mind… entering your stop price into the market also leaves you vulnerable. Investors or brokers who see your stop can manipulate the share price to push you out of the position.

The safest thing to do is track your stops privately. You can do this with a simple excel spreadsheet... or with a service like TradeStops.

— 3 —
Bonds

For many investors, bonds are one of the best investment ideas ever created...

Bond investing is a simple concept.

A business needs to borrow money to fund its operations. The investor has money to lend.

The investor loans the business money. Just like a bank, the investor collects interest payments on the loan... and gets his money back at the end of the agreement.

When an investor loans money to a company, it's called "buying a bond." The company issues the bond. The investor buys it. "Buying a bond" is just another way to say "loaning money."

Bonds are attractive to many investors because companies are contractually obligated to pay the money back. This can result in years of steady interest payments.

It's just like a homeowner borrowing money from a bank. The borrower pays the loan off over years. If he doesn't pay the loan, the bank forecloses on the property.

Many investors like bonds over stocks because bonds offer more safety. When you loan money to a company, it is contractually obligated to pay you interest for as long as it is in business. You don't care about the stock price moving up or down. You just collect your interest every year.

Although bonds are typically safer than stocks, it's still possible to go wrong in this area. That's why it's critical to know the basics here. This section covers them...

———————●———————

Bonds are loans. The organization that issues (sells) the bonds is borrowing money from the buyers. The bond market is larger than the stock market when measured in dollars.

Bonds have three main components: a stated principal, a fixed interest rate, and a fixed maturity. In most cases, these do not change.

Face value: The stated principal. This is what the buyer pays when the bond is issued. And it's what the bondholder receives at maturity.

Fixed interest rate: The bond pays this rate until maturity. This is also known as the coupon rate and nominal yield. It is fixed and does not change.

Fixed maturity: Bonds have a defined life. At maturity, the bond pays the owner the face value.

Here are some other key terms to keep in mind as we explore the world of bonds…

Bond price: Price of a bond in the secondary market. A bond's price may or may not be equal to the face value.

Bond rating: Private companies rate the creditworthiness of bond issuers based on the financial health of the issuer. The higher the rating, the safer the bonds are. (More about ratings later.)

For example, a $10,000 (face value) bond pays 5% (interest rate) and matures in five years. For most bonds, none of these values ever change for the bond's life.

But there are many variations that may not fit this description.

Initial Issue

Bonds are initially issued and sold to the public. They are rated before issue. After that, bonds are traded in the secondary market. No money goes to the bond issuer from sales in the secondary market. The price in the secondary market may or may not be the same as the face value.

The principal or face value is what you pay to buy the bond when it is issued. It may not be what you could sell it for in the secondary market.

Interest Payments

The interest is paid on a regular schedule. Most bonds pay interest twice a year. Others pay quarterly. Some bonds pay no interest until maturity.

For example, a $10,000 bond with an interest rate of 5% pays $500 per year to the bondholder. The bondholder receives two checks of $250 each in the first year.

At the end of five years, the bond matures. At maturity, the bondholder receives the face value of $10,000. The bondholder has earned $2,500 over five years ($500 per year).

Bonds vs. Certificates of Deposit

In some ways, bonds are like bank **certificates of deposit (CDs)**. When you buy a CD, you are lending the bank your money. At the end of a fixed period, you receive the principal back plus interest.

Unlike bonds, you can't readily sell your CD. You will often pay a penalty if you have to get your money out before maturity.

CDs sold by FDIC-insured banks are protected up to $250,000 per depositor. If the bank fails, the FDIC covers the face amount of your CD. Bonds, however, are sold on the credit of the issuer. The better the credit of the issuers, the less interest the bond pays. If the bond issuer fails, you will likely not get refunded at face value.

For example, Detroit went bankrupt in 2013 and owed bond-holders billions of dollars. Bondholders received pennies on the dollar. Some bond issuers buy insurance that assures owners of payments and principal if the issuer is unable to pay out the full amount owed.

Bond investors must be compensated for buying bonds from less creditworthy issuers. These bonds must pay a higher interest rate to attract buyers.

Independent companies rate each bond issuer for creditworthiness. They assign bonds what amounts to a credit score. The score tells investors how risky the bonds are. (More about bond ratings below.)

Role of Bonds in Investing

Bonds play an important role in any long-term investment or short-term trading plan. They serve several purposes:

1. As a buffer to stocks.
2. As a source of income.
3. As a way to preserve capital.

Bonds act as a buffer to the volatility of the stock market. Bonds and stocks often move in different directions in response to economic changes.

When the economy is doing well, investors are attracted to stocks. When the economy is receding, investors are more attracted to bonds.

Changes in the economy have no effect on bond interest payments. However, bond prices may go up or down.

The stock market can be very volatile, even from day to day. As a bondholder, you are somewhat protected from that chaos.

Bonds pay a steady and predictable income as interest payments. Many retirees use bond income to help pay daily expenses. Others reinvest the interest payments from a bond mutual fund or exchange-traded fund (more on this later) back into the bond fund. This allows your money to grow faster by buying more shares of the fund.

These interest payments are a more secure form of income than dividends.

Some common stocks pay dividends, but they are not guaranteed. Dividends may be reduced or eliminated if the company needs cash. Preferred stock pays a fixed dividend and in that way is like a bond.

People in or near retirement often use bonds to preserve principal. They may begin pulling money out of stocks as they approach retirement. They don't want to lose a big piece of their nest egg if the market suffers a major drop.

Many investors around retirement age are less concerned with growth. They are more afraid of loss. Bonds provide some protection against loss that stocks do not.

Buying Bonds

There are two ways to own bonds: individually or by mutual fund. They do not accomplish all of the same goals.

When you own bonds directly, keep in mind...

- You can hold bonds until maturity or trade them.
- You pay no holding costs, but do pay commissions to your broker.
- Many bonds require a large initial purchase.
- Bonds protect your principal.
- Trading bonds carries as much risk as trading stocks.

When you own bonds in mutual funds, keep in mind...

- Professionals manage funds.
- Funds respond to market changes.
- Funds may trigger taxes as they trade bonds.

- Funds charge fees, which will eat into your return.
- Funds have low initial deposits.
- Funds offer a variety of maturities.
- You can lose money.
- Funds that have performed well in the past may not do so in the future.
- It's easier to invest in foreign bonds.

Most investors will find benefits in both forms of ownership. (More about mutual funds and exchange-traded funds later.)

Bonds and Interest Rates

The value of bonds declines as interest rates rise. It increases as interest rates fall. How this affects you as a bondholder depends on your goals…

If you are a buy-and-hold bond investor, rising interest rates make little difference. Your bond still pays the same interest rate. The face value is unaffected. But you do miss out on the higher interest-rate payments of newer bonds.

But if you are a short-term bond trader, rising interest rates reduce the value of your bond. If you want to sell an old bond, you will have to discount it.

Let's go back to our previous example… A bond is issued for $10,000 for five years with a 5% interest rate, paid every six months. Then after the bond is issued, interest rates rise to 6%.

You need to sell this bond. But who would buy it when it is paying 1% below market rates (5% vs. 6%)? You have to sweeten the deal so the buyer gets the market rate (6%).

You can't change the interest rate on the bond. That's fixed at 5%. But you can change the price you will sell the bond for. That will change the effective interest rate or yield.

The annual income (interest) payment of $500 ($10,000 x 5%) must equal a 6% payment. The face value of the bond ($10,000) must be discounted. You find that the $500 rate is equal to 6% on $8,333 ($500 / 6% = $8,333). You must re-duce the price of the bond to $8,333 for it to be attractive. The new owner now earns 6% ($8,333 x 6% = $500).

The buyer paid $8,333. But when the bond matures, he re-ceives the full face value of $10,000 – about 20% more than he paid.

If interest rates go down instead of up, you can sell your bond at a premium.

Bond Yield

Bond yield is a common way to discuss the changes in bond prices. Bond prices are almost always quoted from the sec-ondary market.

As our example above points out, changes in bond prices change the effective interest rate or yield. In that example, the price fell and the yield rose from 5% to 6%.

Bond prices and yields move in opposite directions. When bond prices rise, yields fall. When bond prices fall, yields rise.

Falling prices mean the fixed interest payment is applied to a smaller amount than the face value. This means the same dollar amount payment is a greater percentage. So yields rise when the price falls.

Rising prices mean the same dollar amount payment of interest is applied to a larger number. This results in a lower effective yield.

Bonds and Risk

All bondholders face several types of risk, including:

- Interest rate changes
- Maturities
- Default
- Call provisions

Interest Rate Changes

As we have already noted, rising interest rates drive down bond prices. But there are ways to protect yourself from interest rate increases.

A **bond ladder** is one method to minimize interest rate changes. Here's how it works...

Say you have $50,000 to invest in bonds. You could buy one $50,000 bond, but that offers no protection from interest rate changes. There are two options to make sure you're getting the best rate every year using the bond ladder...

OPTION 1:

You have the $50,000 to invest immediately. But instead of putting it all into one bond, you buy five $10,000 bonds with maturities of one to five years. Your five-year ladder would look like this in year one...

- One-year bond for $10,000
- Two-year bond for $10,000
- Three-year bond for $10,000
- Four-year bond for $10,000
- Five-year bond for $10,000

When the one-year bond matures at the end of the first year, you use the proceeds to buy a five-year bond. Each following year, you buy a new five-year bond with the proceeds of the bond maturing that year.

At the end of five years, you own five of the five-year bonds. One will mature every year. Each year, you use the proceeds to buy another five-year bond. **Every year, you're getting the best rate for that year**. If you're looking for higher rates, you can spread the ladder over 10 years and buy 10-year bonds. Those will pay a higher rate, but carry more risk.

OPTION TWO:

If you do not have the full $50,000 to invest at once – but will have part of that available on a yearly basis – you can use this ladder…

- Year 1 – Buy a five-year bond with the first $10,000
- Year 2 – Buy a five-year bond with the next $10,000
- Year 3 – Buy a five -year bond with the next $10,000
- Year 4 – Buy a five -year bond with the next $10,000
- Year 5 – Buy a five-year bond with the next $10,000

As with Option 1… At the end of five years, you own five of the five-year bonds. One will mature every year. Each year, you use the proceeds to buy another five-year bond. **Every year, you are still getting the best rate for that year**.

If you are looking for higher rates, you can spread the ladder over 10 years and buy 10-year bonds. Those will pay a higher rate, but carry more risk.

Maturity

The length to maturity determines the level of risk in the bond. The longer the bond term, the greater the risk of interest rate changes. Shorter-term bonds are less risky for this reason.

Here are the standard lengths of maturities...

- Short-term – two years or less
- Mid-term – two to 10 years
- Long-term – more than 10 years.

Default

The major risk in owning bonds is **default**. That's when the bond issuer can't pay interest or return all of the face value. Your best protection against default is buying highly rated bonds. Spreading bond buys over different types will also lower risk.

The risk of default is highest in corporate bonds. Munis are next. Treasurys have no risk. The bond you buy should reflect your comfort with risk, return goal, and time needed. A good broker can help find the bond for you.

Call Provisions

Some bonds come with a **call provision**. This allows the bond issuer to buy back the bonds at face value. An issuer might do this if interest rates dropped. They could issue new bonds at a lower rate and pay off the older, high-interest bonds.

The risk is you lose a bond that is paying higher-than-market rates. You receive the face value, but you must reinvest the money at a lower rate. Bonds with call provisions should pay slightly more interest for the extra risk.

❀ Rating a Bond

Bond risk is complex to analyze. Investors turn to ratings services to gauge the risk in each bond. *The higher the risk of default, the higher the interest rate the bond pays.* There are three major companies that rate most bonds...

1. Moody's Investors Service
2. Standard & Poor's
3. Fitch Ratings

Most bond issues are rated. Large investors – such as pension funds, insurance companies, and so on – usually will not buy unrated bonds. A bond issue may be unrated because the issuer is not creditworthy. Most, but not all, bond defaults are from unrated bonds. **So if one of the three major ratings services does not rate the bond you want, play it safe and look for another bond**.

Here is an explanation of the credit-worthy rankings these companies give to bonds. The groupings are mine, but roughly equal to what the companies say...

Investment Grade

Moody's – Aaa: These bonds are of the best quality. They carry the smallest degree of risk. Interest payments are protected by an exceptionally stable margin, and principal is secure.

Moody's – Aa, A: These bonds are of high quality by all standards. Margins of protection may not be as large as in Aaa securities.

Moody's – Baa: These bonds possess many favorable investment attributes. Factors giving security to principal and interest are considered adequate.

Standard & Poor's (S&P) – AAA: The issuer's capacity to meet its financial obligation is extremely strong.

S&P – AA, A: The issuer's capacity to meet its financial obligation is very strong.

S&P – BBB, BBB: Although these bonds are somewhat more susceptible to the adverse effects of changing economic conditions, the issuer's capacity to meet its financial obligations is strong.

Fitch – AAA: The best-quality companies, reliable and stable.

Fitch – AA: Quality companies, a bit higher risk than AAA.

Fitch – A: Economic situation can affect finances.

Fitch – BBB: Medium-class companies, which are satisfactory at the moment.

Medium Grade

Moody's – Ba, B: The bonds lack outstanding investment characteristics and have speculative characteristics as well.

S&P – BB+, BB, B: Adverse economic conditions are more likely to lead to a weakened capacity of the issuer to meet its financial commitment.

Fitch – BB, B: More prone to changes in the economy.

You should avoid any bond rated below a "B" until you are an experienced investor.

Remember… a bond's rating can change at any time if circumstances change. The services can lower the rating if some adverse condition arises.

Types of Bonds

There are three main types of bonds. They are:

1. U.S. Treasury/Agency bonds
2. Municipal bonds
3. Corporate bonds

Each type of bond has a particular set of characteristics. This gives the bond buyer a wide choice to meet a variety of needs.

U.S. Treasury/Agency Bonds

U.S. Treasury bond issues are the safest investment you can make. The "full faith and credit" of the U.S. government backs these debts.

Very high safety means a very low return. All interest earned from U.S. Treasury issues is generally exempt from state and local taxes, but not federal income tax.

Here are the different types of U.S. Treasury issues:

Treasury bonds: Have a maturity exceeding 10 years. The Treasury issues them in denominations ranging from $1,000 to $1 million. New 30-year bonds are sold quarterly. They are popular with large institutional investors.

They pay interest every six months. If you buy them on the secondary market, they are still backed by the "full faith and credit" of the U.S. government.

Treasury notes: Have maturities of two, three, five, or 10 years and denominations of $1,000. The U.S. Treasury sells notes at public auction periodically. The interest rate for the note is set at the auction.

The 10-year note is most often cited when discussing the U.S. Treasury bond market. It is closely tied to the 30-year home-mortgage rate.

Treasury bills: Not bonds in the strict sense because their maturities range from four to 26 weeks. T-Bills should be classified as cash management, rather than strictly as "bonds." T-Bills are sold at a discount to face value. At maturity, you receive the face value. The difference is your interest earned.

Because of their short maturities, they are considered the safest of all investment choices.

Treasury Inflation-Protected Securities (TIPS): Bonds with maturities of five, 10, and 20 years. They are sold in $1,000 denominations at auction just like Treasury notes.

TIPS are adjusted for inflation. Every six months, the Treasury adjusts the principal by the Consumer Price Index for inflation. The fixed rate of interest is applied to this inflation-adjusted principal.

In an inflationary environment, every six-month interest payment could be higher than the next. At maturity, the TIPS pays the inflation-adjusted principal or the original face value, whichever is greater.

Organizations related to the U.S. government also issue bonds called **agency bonds**. The largest of the agencies sell bonds backed by home-mortgage loans. Agency bonds pay a higher rate since they are tied to the mortgage industry. Many of these bonds require an initial minimum investment of $25,000.

You can buy U.S. Treasury and Agency products directly from the Treasury or through your bank or other financial institution. The U.S. Treasury website has complete information on all of their products.

Municipal Bonds

Governmental units such as states, counties, and cities issue municipal bonds. The bonds are known as munis for short. They are a popular investment with large institutional investors.

Municipal bonds are generally bought in $5,000 units. In many cases, the minimum is $25,000.

Most munis are exempt from federal income tax. This makes them attractive to high-income investors. In some cases, bond income payments may be exempt from state and local taxes also.

Most municipal bonds mature in a five- to 20-year period. However, you can find longer and shorter maturities.

There are two types of municipal bonds:

1. General obligation bonds
2. Revenue bonds

General obligation bonds are backed by the full faith and credit of the issuing authority. This means the issuer pledges tax resources to pay off the bond.

General obligation bonds pay a slightly higher interest rate than Treasury issues. They are rated on the credit-worthiness of the issuer. Proceeds from the bonds are used to build roads, utilities, and other improvements.

Revenue bonds are used to build projects that will create a revenue stream. Toll roads are a good example of using revenue bonds. Tolls collected are used to retire the bonds. However, the issuer does not back revenue bonds with tax revenue. This makes them more risky than general obligation bonds.

To buy a municipal bond, you will need a stockbroker who specializes in them. Most large brokers have this capability. You describe the type of bond you're looking for and the broker will find one that matches. These bonds are bought in the secondary market. Many large brokers buy blocks of bonds to sell in smaller units to individuals.

A private insurance company insures some municipal bonds. The policy guarantees bondholders they will be paid even if the issuer defaults. Default is not common for munis, but it does happen.

Insured muni bonds receive high ratings. The issuer can offer a lower interest rate with this security.

Corporate Bonds

Companies issue bonds to pay for a variety of projects. Some uses for bonds include:

- Buildings and machinery
- Acquisitions
- Research

Corporate bonds are the most risky of all bond types. They are issued based on the financial strength of the company. Bonds from mature, successful companies carry low risks. Bonds from companies with less than good financial health may be very risky.

Ratings of the bonds are very important in judging risk. The lower-rated the bond, the higher interest rate it pays. However, lower ratings also mean a greater risk of default.

Corporate bonds often come in $1,000 units. They are actively traded in the secondary market. Your stockbroker can help you find the bond you want. You can find a variety of ratings, maturities, and interest rates. You can take as much or as little risk as you want.

Convertible Bonds

Some corporate bonds have a feature that lets you convert the bond into stock. **Convertible bonds** are appealing, especially if you think the company will do well in the future.

The bondholder can convert the bond to stock based on the share price hitting a specified mark. A formula for how and why you can convert the bond to stock is spelled out when the bonds are issued.

The convertible features are part of the bond package. You should understand them completely before buying a convertible bond.

Convertible bonds often pay a slightly lower rate. The feature is an added benefit that pays off if the company does well.

The bond market is huge and diverse. This description only scratches the surface. As you become more experienced with bonds, new possibilities will present themselves.

— 4 —
Mutual Funds

Let's say you want to invest in the stock market... but you don't have the time or the interest to follow individual companies.

Or maybe you've heard that owning a basket of 20 or 30 stocks is safer than owning just one or two stocks.

This is where the last two major investing tools – mutual funds and exchange-traded funds (ETFs) – can come in handy.

The concept behind these investment vehicles is simple: A large group of investors pool their money together. A professional money manager invests that pool of money into a variety of stocks and bonds. He collects a fee for his services. The investors get a diversified basket of investments.

Like any investment vehicle, mutual funds and ETFs can make great sense. But they can also have substantial pitfalls.

In this chapter, you'll learn the basics of mutual funds... their potential benefits... and the dangers to avoid.

Mutual funds may be the most popular form of investing in the U.S. If you have a retirement plan such as a 401(k), you most likely invest in mutual funds. They are a convenient way for many investors to put money away each month or each paycheck...

Mutual funds are simply a way investors can pool their money. Professional money managers invest the pool of money. Mutual funds have goals and objectives to help investors decide if the fund is right for them...

For example, you can find mutual funds that invest only in growth stocks. Other funds may invest for income and choose mature, large companies that pay a consistent dividend. There are bond funds and hybrids that combine stocks and bonds.

You decide what your investment goals are and find a mutual fund that matches your needs.

There are thousands of mutual funds to choose from. According to one count, there are more than 10,000. You can find a mutual fund for just about any investing strategy. Most mutual funds invest in stocks and/or bonds. There are four broad categories of mutual funds:

- Stock funds
- Bond funds
- Combination (of stocks and bonds) funds
- Money market funds

Other funds invest in real estate, precious metals, and other securities.

Every mutual fund has a prospectus. The prospectus outlines the fund's investment objectives and fees. Fund managers often have wide choices in investment decisions. For example, a mutual fund that invests in small companies may also invest in larger companies, options, or other securities. Fund managers may vary from main objectives to help increase fund performance.

It is the manager's job to invest the fund's money for the best possible return. They buy and sell stocks (or bonds) to meet the fund's objectives.

How well the fund performs is a matter of public record. It is easy to see the fund's track record over its life. This gives you a picture of how it performed in different market conditions. However, the main warning about all funds is "past performance is no guarantee of future results."

Mutual Funds vs. Stocks

Mutual funds differ from stocks, bonds, and most other securities in several major ways. We'll look at the top three…

The first difference is that in most cases, investors buy "shares" of mutual funds directly from the fund. That means you don't need a stockbroker to buy into a mutual fund. You contact the fund directly and open an account. You can do this by phone or online with most funds.

Second, investors buy in dollar amounts rather than share counts. Most funds have a modest minimum initial investment. You can add to your account in almost any dollar amount you want. Your investment is converted to whole and fractional shares. For example, you might own 25.3987 shares of the fund. We'll look at how shares are defined in more detail later.

Third, you can't buy and sell fund shares during the trading day. Mutual funds must wait until the markets close before re-calculating how much shares are worth. The value will change depending on how the fund's investments did that day.

Advantages of Mutual Funds

The main advantage of investing in mutual funds is the professional management. Few individual investors can afford a private money manager. With mutual funds, you not only get a manager, but you also get a team of analysts and other money professionals. It's their job to produce the best results possible for the fund.

Fund managers are paid a fee based on the amount of money invested and other considerations. If they guide the fund to a great return, more people will invest. They earn more as the fund grows. So they're personally interested in the fund performing well. However, they are paid a fee regardless of how the fund performs.

Funds may also have a level of diversification most individuals can't match. For example, you may want some of your money in large-cap stocks...

A large-cap stock fund may own 50 or more different stocks. This spreads out the risk over many companies, which would be impossible for an individual. If one stock in the fund collapses, it will have minimal impact on the fund.

Disadvantages of Mutual Funds

One of the biggest flaws of mutual funds is their fees.

Investors in the fund pay certain fees. Depending on the fund, these fees may be small or large. The fund manager collects the fees each year. The fees are not tied to fund performance. Even in a bad year, investors pay the fees.

Fees reduce investors' returns. The higher the fees, the less you earn. Or in a bad year, the more you lose. An often-quoted statistic is that 80% of the funds with high fees fail to beat the S&P 500 each year. (More about fees later.)

Another disadvantage of mutual funds is that it's hard for anyone to consistently pick good investments. A poor (or unlucky) money manager may not add any value to the fund. Some investment styles work well when the markets are operating a certain way. When those conditions change, the same investment style may be a disaster.

This is one reason to look at the fund's returns over a long period. How did the fund do in a good market? What about in a bad market or a flat market? Also, how consistent is the management from year to year?

Mutual funds may also fall victim to market extremes. When you invest in a mutual fund, the manger must put that money to use. If the market is booming, a lot of people may want to invest in the fund. Investing this new money can drive up the price of securities by increasing demand. And the fund pays more for the securities.

If the market suffers a serious dip, some investors will want to pull their money out. The fund manager must sell securities to generate the cash to buy back their investment.

The fund manager may be forced to sell securities she would prefer to hold in order to pay investors. This selling can drive down prices even further.

Understanding NAV

Mutual funds are sold based on a number called the **net asset value (NAV)**. This number roughly relates to a share price. You can own fractions of shares.

The NAV represents the value of the underlying securities minus liabilities and fees and divided by the number of shares. As these prices rise or fall, so does the NAV. The NAV is calculated at the market close every day.

For example, a mutual fund has a NAV of $39.75. If you open an account with $2,000, you have bought 50.314 shares. The next week, the fund's NAV is $41.25. Your stake in the fund is now worth $2,075.49. Here it is in a table:

No. of Shares	NAV	Dollar Value
50.314	$39.75	$2,000.00
50.314	$41.25	$2.075.29

You have earned about $75.29 on your investment without buying any additional shares.

If you want to invest more money or sell some shares, it is done at the NAV computed that day. For example, if you want to sell (or "redeem") $2,000 on Monday, the NAV computed Monday would be the price you receive. Same with buying. If you want to buy $1,000 of shares on Monday, the fund uses the NAV computed after the markets close Monday.

Open-End Funds

Most mutual funds are **open-end funds**. This means the fund can issue as many shares as it wants based on investor demand. This type of fund also buys back shares when investors want to sell.

Open-end funds don't trade on stock exchanges. You can only buy or sell funds to the mutual fund. When investors want to buy shares, the fund issues new ones. When investors want to sell, the fund buys back the shares.

Closed-End Funds

A small number of funds are closed-end funds. They are not like open-end funds or a typical mutual fund. A **closed-end fund** often has a static portfolio of securities. Closed-end funds raise money with an initial public offering of a limited number of shares.

Once the closed-end fund is sold out, it is listed on a stock exchange. Unlike other mutual funds, it trades like a stock. Its price rises and falls based on supply and demand. Owning shares in a closed-end fund is more like owning stock than a typical mutual fund.

Fund Management

Mutual funds have one of two basic management styles: actively managed and passively managed.

Actively managed funds have a management team that buys and sells securities to get the best return for the investor. During any year, they may turn over 100% of the portfolio. Some actively managed funds do well. But most struggle to meet their investment goals. The primary reason for this is they charge high fees. These fees can be 2%-plus per year.

Passively managed funds seldom change the contents of their portfolios. Most often, these funds track an index of securities.

For example, one of the most popular indexes is the S&P 500. There are several mutual funds that track this index. Their investment goal is to match the performance of the S&P 500. They buy the same stocks that are in the S&P 500.

Some passively managed funds do not duplicate the index, but copy in substance the major components.

Passively managed funds are most noted for their low fees. Some of the funds have fees as low as 0.25% per year. These funds do as well as the indexes they track.

Types of Mutual Funds

Mutual funds are defined by the type of securities they hold and by their investment strategies.

It is important to remember that even though a fund calls itself a "stock fund," for example, it may also invest in other securities.

The major type of funds defined by their portfolios include...

Stock funds invest primarily in common stock.

Bond funds invest primarily in bonds. However, they often specialize in one type of bond. For example, a bond fund may invest solely in highly rated corporate bonds.

Balanced funds often combine stocks and bonds in differing percentages. These fund managers may move more assets into stocks if that's where the best return is. Or they can shift assets into bonds to take advantage of an upswing in the bond market.

Index funds track various stock and bond indexes. There are hundreds of indexes that track different aspects of the stock and bond markets. You can find an index fund for almost all these indexes. Exchange-traded funds – which we'll talk about in the next chapter – also track various indexes.

Sector funds invest in narrow sectors of the stock and bond markets. These funds let you buy a strong presence in those sectors if you feel they will grow faster than the whole market.

Foreign funds (or "global funds") invest in foreign stocks and bonds. Some funds count U.S. companies with major global markets as foreign stocks. Other funds invest in strictly foreign stocks and bonds. They often focus in a particular area of the global economy.

Commodity funds focus on commodities or groups of commodities by buying stocks and bonds in producing companies. These funds often specialize in or include oil, coal, gold, and other natural resources. Some commodity funds invest in derivatives, such as futures contracts. We will look at the futures market in a later section.

Money market funds invest in cash-equivalent securities such as short-term U.S. Treasury bills. Investors often park money in these funds while waiting for an investment opportunity.

Precious-metal funds focus on precious metals such as gold and silver. They may own stocks in companies that mine, refine, or process the metals.

Mutual-Fund Strategies

You can also define mutual funds by their investment strategy. This is helpful in finding funds that match your strategy. You must use caution, however, in picking funds based on strategy.

A fund's name may or may not describe its investment strategy. Acme Growth Fund may actually invest in some stocks that are not growth stocks. The fund does this to help it reach investment targets.

A "growth" fund that invests mainly in large, well-established companies is not a growth fund. The same caution applies for all strategy funds.

Growth funds aim for much higher returns than the broad market. They invest in high-growth companies and sectors. They might be heavily invested in small technology companies, for example. These funds take more risks in looking for higher rewards. They either do great or terrible.

Value funds invest in securities the market has not priced correctly. Value investing is a long-term strategy that can be very profitable. For example, the fund buys a stock that is priced less than its true value. When the market corrects the stock's price by bidding it up, the fund has a profit.

Blended funds combine growth and value strategies. The blend of value and growth stocks often reduces some of the risk in growth funds. It also has potentially greater returns than a pure value fund. Another type of blended fund invests in a combination of stocks and bonds.

Leveraged funds borrow money to increase potential returns. They are complex funds that may track certain stock indexes. The use of leverage (borrowed money) increases gains, but also may result in significant losses.

Some stock funds focus on companies of a certain size as measured by market cap. Most investors like to spread their investments across companies of all sizes. You can find funds that focus on small-, mid-, and large-cap stocks.

Fund Expenses

All mutual funds charge investors fees to manage their money. The more managed the fund is, the higher the fees. Stocks you buy directly from the fund usually have lower fees than those you buy from a broker.

Management Fees

Management fees pay for:

- The fund manager and staff
- Administrative costs to run the fund (utilities, rent, and so on)
- Advertising and sales expenses

For actively managed funds, these costs can be high. Talented managers and researchers must be paid. For passively managed funds, these fees should be much lower.

These total fees are often called the expense ratio. Funds with higher expense ratios must perform even better to compensate for the fees. But most studies conclude *funds with high expense ratios do not produce better returns.* In fact, just the opposite is the case.

Loads

There are two broad types of funds defined by the fees they charge:

- No-load funds
- Loaded funds

The term "**load**" in this context means fees paid to sales-people. All funds charge a management fee. However, some funds also charge a fee that is a commission to the broker for selling the fund.

No-load funds do not charge this fee. You can buy shares directly from the mutual fund. Loaded funds charge a per-centage of your purchase to pay the salesperson. There is no evidence these funds perform better than no-load funds.

Picking a Mutual Fund

There are thousands of mutual funds. Financial-services site Morningstar has extensive information on mutual funds. Much is free, although its best information is for paid subscribers.

Taxes

One of the downsides of mutual funds – especially actively managed funds – is taxes. As the fund buys and sells securities, it creates tax bills. These bills are passed to the shareholders.

If the security sold for a profit was held by the fund less than one year, the tax is a short-term capital gain. These taxes are treated like ordinary income to the shareholder.

If the security is held for longer than one year, the taxes are long-term capital gains. These gains may be taxed at a lower rate than ordinary income.

— 5 —

Exchange-Traded Funds

So far, we've learned about stocks, bonds, and mutual funds. Now we'll look at the newest of the four major investing tools: Exchange-traded funds (ETFs).

ETFs combine features of mutual funds and stocks. They let you buy a basket of stocks or bonds with one purchase. They're similar to index mutual funds. However, you buy and sell ETFs just like stocks in the market.

These funds represent an undivided interest in a basket of assets. The assets are held "in trust" at the creation of the fund. A share of an ETF represents an ownership in this basket of assets. An ETF is created when a large number of the assets (stocks or bonds, for example) are deposited in the trust.

The basket can be stocks or bonds or other securities. You can find ETFs for almost any investing strategy.

Not all ETFs track market indexes. For example, the SPDR Gold Trust Fund holds gold in trust. You can track the ETF using the symbol GLD.

Unlike other ETFs, shares of GLD represent an undivided share of ownership in gold. This ETF mimics the price of gold bullion on the open market.

You can also buy a number of gold mutual funds, although most of these track gold and mining stocks and bonds.

———————●———————

Bond ETFs

Many investors want to own bonds, but it is often difficult and expensive. There are a number of **bond ETFs** that track various bond indexes or specialize in a certain type of bond.

They are much like bond mutual funds. They distribute income and dividends to owners. And they both resolve the issue of buying municipal bonds in large denominations, since you are buying into the fund rather than the bond directly.

An ETF makes it easy to get into and out of the bond market, since you can trade them during market hours.

However, neither a bond mutual fund nor an ETF acts just like a bond. If your goal is to preserve capital, mutual funds and ETFs may not be for you. You can lose money investing in either.

Sector ETFs

Sector ETFs let you zero in on a part of the stock market that you believe is moving in one direction or the other. For example, if you think the technology sector is about to rise dramatically, you buy an ETF that tracks technology or parts of the sector.

This ability to focus on a slice of the market makes ETFs popular with traders looking for short-term gains in the sector.

Some of the sector funds include:

- Global ETFs
- Real estate ETFs
- Precious-metals ETFs
- Derivative ETFs
- Exotic ETFs

Most of these sector funds cover stocks or bonds. There are some more exotic ETFs that invest in commodities and other derivatives. (More about these in the next section.) Other ETFs use borrowed money to increase returns. This also increases the risk.

Exotic ETFs are not suited for beginning investors because it may be difficult to determine the actual risk of the products.

ETFs vs. Mutual Funds

ETFs and index mutual funds share much in common. Both track major stock and bond indexes. Both offer investments focused in particular areas of the market.

Both products have advantages and disadvantages. It is sometimes difficult to compare mutual funds and ETFs on performance. The S&P 500 Index comes the closest...

Performance

The S&P 500 Index is the most followed stock market indicator. As its name suggests, it is made up of 500 stocks.

The SPDR S&P 500 ETF (SPY) tracks this popular index. You could also buy shares of an S&P 500 Index mutual fund. One of the most popular is Vanguard 500 Index Fund Investor Shares (VFINX).

Using Morningstar.com's numbers for total return, the two are virtually identical going back 15 years. The difference in total return was only a few hundreds of a percentage point.

This may not be true when comparing other mutual funds and ETFs.

Ease of Purchase

You don't usually pay a commission to buy a mutual fund, but there are ongoing expenses. Expenses for an ETF are usually much lower. But you must pay a commission each time you buy or sell.

Once you open a mutual-fund account, you can make regular deposits of amounts as low as $25 per month. Each fund has its own opening deposit and ongoing deposit requirements.

If your goal is to invest over time, a mutual fund probably makes more sense.

Trading

You buy and sell ETFs just like stocks in the market. There is no limit to the number of times you can buy or sell an ETF. Of course, you will pay a commission to your broker each time you trade.

You can trade mutual funds. But they only sell or buy (redeem) shares after the market closes. Many mutual funds actively discourage trading. Some may penalize you for too many trades.

You can use the same trading tactics with ETFs that are used with stocks. You can purchase options on most ETFs.

If your goal is short-term trading profits, ETFs are the better choice. You can also hold ETFs for long-term gains.

Taxes

ETFs are generally more tax-friendly than mutual funds. Actively managed mutual funds buy and sell securities during the year. These capital gains (and losses) are passed to the shareholders.

Dividends from mutual funds and ETFs are taxed. There are special rules for how long you must own the ETF that determine how dividends are taxed.

Taxes are complicated. The rules change constantly, so consult a qualified tax expert with questions.

ETF Investing Strategies

You can use many of the same investing strategies available to stocks and bonds. This flexibility makes them attractive to investors.

You can use these strategies to:

- Trade short-term trends
- Invest in sectors, precious metals, or other areas of the market
- Hold for longer-term gains
- Diversify your portfolio

— 6 —

Options, Futures, Currencies, and Others

As we've discussed, the four basic investment tools are stocks, bonds, mutual funds, and exchange-traded funds.

You can build a successful investment program with one or more of these tools. Most investors don't need or want to use any other strategies.

But for those who are interested, we'll now review some of the more advanced trading choices in the market. We'll briefly look at…

1. Call and put options.
2. Futures contracts.
3. Currency trading.

These choices are not for beginning investors.

Before we start, a word about risk: These trading choices are much riskier than stocks, bonds, or funds. You can lose all the money you put into them. So make sure you use exit strategies and consult a professional before using any of these strategies.

Derivatives

A **derivative** is a contract for an asset between a buyer and seller. Most commonly, you agree to buy or sell an asset for a certain price during a certain period.

This is a security that is priced in part based on an underlying asset. As the price of the asset changes, the price of the derivative changes. Supply and demand also influence the derivative's price.

A common derivative is an **option**. Options are used to generate additional income in the markets.

There are two kinds of options – **call options** and **put options**.

And there are two sides to each options trade – you can either buy or sell the option.

As the buyer of a call or put option, you profit if the stock price goes the direction you anticipate. You can then sell the option at the higher price and pocket the difference.

As a seller of call or put options, you profit if the stock price goes the direction you anticipate. You keep the money you collected from selling the option whether it moves in the right direction or not.

So What Is An Option?

Options are suitable for many investors *after some experience in the market*. They are not for beginners.

Options are derivatives that primarily use stocks or exchange-traded funds as the underlying asset. You can also trade options on major market indexes.

As we said, each option has a buyer and a seller. You can conduct your options trades in a regular brokerage account. But you have to meet certain requirements to trade options.

If you plan to trade options, your broker will require you to sign a special **options agreement**. It spells out your responsibilities.

Your broker will ask you questions to determine your knowledge of options trading. If the broker determines you don't have enough experience, he may not allow you to trade certain types of option strategies. Your broker may also require a minimum deposit before opening an options account.

Each call and put option states the rights and obligations of the buyer and the seller. It states a certain action, at a certain price, for a certain time period. The seller is the only obligated party in an option contract.

We'll talk about calls and puts in more detail in a minute. But first, there are several key terms we need to understand...

Key terms

Call-option buyer: Has the right, but not the obligation, to buy the stock at a certain price by a certain date.

Call-option seller: Has the obligation to sell the stock at the strike price before the expiration date if the buyer exercises the option.

Put-option buyer: Has the right, but not the obligation, to sell the stock at a certain price by a certain date.

Put-option seller: Has the obligation to buy the stock at a certain price by a certain date.

Premium: The price an option buyer pays. It is quoted on a per-share basis. Options are traded in 100-share lots, so you pay 100 times the quoted premium.

Exercise: To put into effect the right specified in the contract. For instance, the option buyer can "exercise" his right to buy shares at the strike price.

Strike price: The price at which the option can be exercised. It is part of the option quote.

Expiration date: The date when the option ends or expires. Option contracts generally expire on the third Friday of each month.

Call Option

A call option gives the buyer the right to buy a stock at a certain price during the life of the option. **You buy a call option if you believe the price of the stock will rise**. Three things can happen if you buy a call option:

1. **The stock price rises**. The call owner must sell you the stock at the lower strike price. Or you can sell the option, which will rise in price with the stock.
2. **The stock price stays the same**. The option expires worthless, and you lose the premium.
3. **The stock price falls**. The option expires worthless, and you lose the premium.

Here is an example of a winning call-option trade…

The stock price is $20 per share. You buy a call option for $2 with a strike price of $20. *You're betting the price of the stock will rise and you can buy shares for cheap.*

The $2 you paid for the call is the "option premium." Remember… options are traded in 100-share lots. That makes the option premium of our sample trade $200.

Before option-expiration day, the stock rises to $25. Your call option is now worth $7 per share. You sell the call, which gives you a $5-per-share profit.

Put Option

A put option gives the buyer the right to sell a stock at a certain price during the life of the option. **You buy a put option if you believe the price of the stock will fall**. Three things can happen if you buy a put option:

1. **The stock falls in price**. You sell the option for a profit. The put's price will rise as the stock's price falls.
2. **The stock price stays the same**. The option expires worthless, and you lose the premium.
3. **The stock price rises**. The option expires worthless, and you lose the premium.

Here is an example of a winning put-option trade:

The stock price is $20 per share. You buy a put option with a strike price of $20.

Like in our call example, the option premium is $2 per share ($200 per contract).

Before option-expiration day, the stock price falls to $15. The option is now worth $7 per share, giving you a $5-per-share profit when you sell.

Are Options Risky?

They can be. As noted above, three things can happen when you buy an option. Two of those end with you losing your premium. There is a greater risk in some of the more exotic trading strategies, but loss of premium is the main risk.

If you buy 100 shares of a stock outright for $20 – rather than trading options on the stock – you will pay $2,000. It is unlikely the price will go to $0 per share before you can sell. So your downside is limited.

If you buy a call option for $200, it is possible to lose the entire amount. But you also have high upside. **These trading strategies are for experienced traders only**.

Futures Contracts

Futures contracts are like options, but with some important differences.

Like an option, a futures contract is between two investors. Each futures contract outlines the rights and obligations of each party. *Unlike options, both parties in a futures contract are bound to fill the terms unless they close their positions.*

For example… if you buy a futures contract, you are obligated to buy the asset at the stated price. If you sell the futures contract, you are obligated to sell the asset at the stated price.

In actual practice, most futures contracts are never completed. A buyer or seller can close his position by buying the opposite side of the contract. If you bought a futures contract for 5,000 bushels of wheat, you could close the position by selling the same contract with the same delivery date and price. This effectively zeros out your position.

Buyers and Sellers of Futures Contracts

The buyer agrees to buy the asset at the agreed price on or before expiration. The seller agrees to sell the asset at the specified price on or before expiration.

There is a futures market for assets such as…

- Wheat
- Corn
- Orange juice
- Pork
- Gold
- Silver
- Financial instruments
- Equity indexes

Some assets call for physical delivery. Others are settled in cash. In actual practice, few futures contracts go to settlement. Buyers and sellers offset their position by buying the other side of the contract. If you are a buyer, you sell the same contract. If you are a seller, you buy the same contract. In both cases, you void your responsibilities.

You would exit the trade if it wasn't going your way – if the price of the asset was moving away from your position.

Futures Players

Two types of investors buy or sell futures contracts: producers/users and speculators.

The main difference is that producers and users hedge against future price changes. Speculators hope to profit off price changes.

Here's an example of hedging… If you grow wheat, you can use futures contracts to lock in a price before the crop is harvested. If your company uses wheat in its product, you can lock in a price for future supplies. In both cases, you are hedging against future price changes.

Margin

Futures contracts are bought with a small cash outlay compared to the total value of a contract. This deposit is called the **initial margin**.

For example, you might deposit $5,000 to buy a contract for a $100,000 asset. Like options, price changes in the underlying asset affect the value of the futures contract. Since the contracts are highly leveraged, a small movement in the underlying price can have a major impact on the contract's value.

You are required to maintain a certain balance as specified by your broker. Futures contracts are settled daily. If your position loses value in daily trading, that amount is deducted from the initial margin. If losses reduce your account below the maintenance level, you are expected to deposit enough in the account (daily) to raise it to that level.

Trading Futures

Trading futures is complicated and risky for the novice investor. Study all you can about the market and asset you want to trade. The futures market has its own rules and quirks that can trap the unwary.

The Commodities Futures Trading Commission (CFTC) is charged with regulating the industry. You can read more about the rules for trading futures on the CFTC website: http://www.cftc.gov/index.htm.

There are many ways to participate in the futures market. You can open an account with a professional trader who will manage trading for you. Or you can invest through indirect ways like futures mutual funds, options, and exchange-traded funds. These familiar products eliminate the risk of directly investing in futures contracts.

What's the Risk?

If you are directly trading contracts, you should beware the cost of mistakes. You can lose the initial deposit… and much more.

Trading futures contracts is not for the novice investor. More advanced investors should allocate only a small percentage of their investing capital in futures (if at all). Be sure you know the potential loss you face if things go badly.

Currency Trading

Currency trading is the largest market in the world. Daily trading volume is in the trillions of dollars. The foreign exchange market is known as **forex (FX)**.

Most of the forex trading is done for speculative purposes. Hedge funds, large institutional investors, and individuals trade currencies.

Opening an account is easy and tempting because of the possible large payoffs. The tremendous leverage of forex trading means a small investment can result in a big gain if your trade is successful.

The major difference between forex trading and the stock market is forex trading is largely unregulated. There are few restrictions in opening an account and plenty of action. The forex trades around the clock with only a brief break on the weekend.

The basics of forex trading are simple. Currencies fluctuate in value compared to other currencies. Changes in interest rates and other economic news can shift these values. When the value of the U.S. dollar falls, the value of other currencies rises.

You trade the forex in pairs of currencies. For example, the EUR/USD pairs the euro and the U.S. dollar. A **forex quote** is always the first currency compared to the second. Quotes are noted to four decimal points. A EUR/USD quote of 1.3723 means one euro equals 1.3723 U.S. dollars.

You simultaneously buy one currency and sell the other. If you expect one currency to rise in value, you buy it and sell the other part of the pair. If the trade goes as expected, you reverse the buy and sell to exit the trade. You profit on the difference.

Forex trading is highly leveraged, which means it's possible to make a lot of money or lose a lot of money quickly. Leverage of 50-to-1 is the norm. This means for every $1 invested, $50 are leveraged. Retail traders compete with professional traders in the market, so arm yourself with as much information as possible.

Forex trading is another avenue for more adventurous investors. But nobody really knows what direction a currency will move. So due to the potential for loss, limit the amount you invest to a tiny percentage of your capital.

For the vast majority of folks out there, it's best to pass on currency trading.

Key Economic Terminology

Once you start investing, you're bound to read financial articles in newspapers like the *Wall Street Journal*.

You might start watching some financial television.

In these places, you'll come across terms like "GDP" and "consumer confidence." These are terms that describe aspects of the economy.

In this section, we'll cover key economic terms you'll see in the paper or hear about on television.

It's good to know what these terms mean. But don't worry about following them closely. Achieving investment success doesn't require being an expert on the economy. It's much more important to focus on getting value for your investment dollar and avoiding big risks.

Still, it's good to know what all this stuff means…

Gross domestic product (GDP): The value of the economy's output. When the GDP is growing, the economy is healthy. When the growth of the GDP slows or stops, the economy may be in trouble.

A GDP growth rate of 3% or so is considered a healthy increase. If the economy is not growing this fast, the unemployment rate rises. However, if the GDP grows faster, it creates inflation.

Recession: Marks a decline in the GDP. It is generally measured by two quarters of negative GDP growth. The government reacts by lowering interest rates and increasing spending. The stock market often reacts with falling stock prices.

Depression: Marks a decline of 10% or more in the GDP along with a recession lasting more than two years.

The U.S. economy has not suffered a depression since the 1920s. Many believe we can avoid a depression. Others are not convinced.

Key economic reports: Government reports issued on important indicators about the health of the economy. Investors should know what these indicators mean.

Consumer price index (CPI): Measures household spending. The change in the CPI is known as inflation. Higher inflation means the dollar buys less.

The traditional cure for inflation is higher interest rates.

Consumer confidence: Tells us how people feel about spending. If they are confident, people spend more. Spending drives the economy up. People cut spending if they are concerned about the economy.

Unemployment (Jobs): The number of employed people is an important economic indicator. There are fewer jobless people in an expanding economy and more in a contracting one.

High unemployment means consumers are not spending money at a rate that boosts the economy.

Durable goods: Items that last more than three years. Cars and major appliances are durable goods.

A healthy economy will buy more durable goods. That means more jobs for people who make and sell durable goods.

New factory orders: A rise or fall in factory orders indicates the rate of economic growth. More new factory orders suggests the economy is growing. The Commerce Department reports on the number of new factory orders. The report is more detailed than the durable-goods report.

Interest rates: The Federal Reserve Board (the Fed) sets interest rates. Its actions affect both what you pay for a loan and what you receive for a savings investment. The Fed sets the most basic interest rate. This interest rate is used to set almost all other interest rates in the economy.

The Fed also has the unique ability to "print money." If the economy is in trouble, the Fed can add money into circulation. This can help banks meet emergency needs in times of crisis.

Lower interest rates help economic expansion. Adding money to the economy helps keep the financial system stable.

Lower interest rates and expanding money supplies can also create inflation. The Fed must walk a line between too much stimulus and not enough.

Investors watch the Fed for signs of increasing or decreasing interest rates. Interest rates have a direct impact on stocks and especially bonds.

If You're Interested in More Knowledge...

At Stansberry Research, we know starting out as an investor can be intimidating.

Spend a few minutes in the investment section of a bookstore or watch a financial television program, and you'll encounter at least a dozen market strategies and "gurus." It's information overload.

If you're new to investing – or new to the Stansberry Research family – it can be overwhelming. We feature numerous investment experts... each with their own strategies and beliefs.

Although our research products feature different styles of investing, all our services are rooted in the same intellectual principles. We believe these principles are vital to successful wealth-building.

You'll find an excellent introduction to these principles in our book *The Stansberry Research Starter's Guide for New Investors*.

In this guide, we've identified the concepts we believe are imperative to successful wealth-building and investment. It's an easy-to-read book that includes descriptions of each concept.

These are the ideas we wish we'd learned before we invested a single dollar.

Becoming a successful investor is a long journey. But reading *The Stansberry Research Starter's Guide for New Investors* will greatly reduce the time it takes to travel it.

You can learn how to get a copy of *The Stansberry Research Starter's Guide for New Investors* by visiting the Stansberry Research Bookstore. You can go to our Bookstore by typing this link into your Internet browser:
http://stansberryresearch.com/bookstore/.

Regards,

Brian Hunt
Editor in Chief
Stansberry Research

Glossary

12b-1 distribution fees: Fees charged to mutual-fund share-holders for advertising and marketing as well as "distribution" costs.

401(k): A retirement plan offered by many employers. The employer may match some portion of the employee's contribution.

52-week range: A stock's highest price and lowest price for the previous 52 weeks of trading.

A

Actively managed mutual funds: Open-end funds that employ a portfolio manager who buys and sells stocks and bonds.

Agency bond: Bond issued by organizations related to the U.S. government. Agency bonds backed by home-mortgage loans pay a higher rate. Denominations of $25,000.

All-or-none order: Order to your broker to either fill the entirety of your order or none of it.

American depositary receipt (ADR): A way to buy shares of some foreign companies.

Annual report: A required document all publicly traded companies must have that presents the financial results for the past fiscal year.

Ask price: The price a seller is willing to accept for a stock.

Assets: What the company owns.

Average volume: Number of shares traded on an average day.

B

Balance sheet: An accounting for a company's assets, liabilities, equity, and net worth at a certain point in time.

Balanced fund: Mutual fund that often combines stocks and bonds in differing percentages, depending on which investment has the best return at that time.

Bear market: When people dump their stocks over an extended period of time... and stock prices fall 20%-plus over a two-month period.

Bid price: The price a buyer is willing to pay for a stock.

Blended fund: Mutual fund that combines growth and value strategies to reduce some of the risk in growth funds.

Blue-chip (core) stock: One of the safest stocks to buy. May not have as big increases or decreases in price as other stocks during big market moves.

Bond: A loan with three main components – stated principal, fixed interest rate, and a fixed maturity.

Bond ETF: Tracks various bond indexes or specializes in a certain type of bond.

Bond fund: Mutual fund that invests primarily in bonds, often specializing in one type of bond.

Bond investing: Investor loans a business money and collects interest payments on that loan, which the business is contractually obligated to pay back.

Bond ladder: One method to minimize interest rate changes.

Bond price: Price of a bond in the secondary market – may or may not be equal to face value.

Bond rating: Private companies rate the creditworthiness of bond issuers based on the financial health of the issuer. The higher the rating, the safer the bond.

Bond yield: The effective interest rate of a bond – moves inversely to the bond price.

Book value: What a company owns minus what it owes.

Book value per share: Book value divided by number of shares.

Bubble: When investors become over confident, prices can rise more than is warranted by the fundamentals. This period of rapid expansion is followed by a massive selloff, which leads to a drastic drop in prices.

Bull market: When there are more buyers than sellers in the market over a long period… and stock prices climb 20%-plus over a two-month period.

Buy-and-hold investing: A strategy of identifying quality investments and holding them rather than actively trading.

C

Call-option buyer: Has the right, but not the obligation, to buy the stock at a certain price by a certain date.

Call-option seller: Has the obligation to sell the stock at the strike price before the expiration date if the buyer exercises the option.

Call provision: Allows the bond issuer to buy back the bonds at face value before maturity if market rates fall.

Cash account: Simplest type of brokerage account.

Certificate of Deposit (CD): Money an investor loans to a bank (similar to a bond). Unlike a bond, you often pay a penalty if you sell your money before maturity.

Closed-end mutual fund: Raises money with an IPO of a limited number of shares. Has a static portfolio of securities.

Closing price: Price point where a stock ends trading for that day.

Common share: A type of security that represents ownership in a corporation. Shareholders get one vote for each share owned.

Commodity fund: Mutual fund that focuses on commodities or groups of commodities by buying stocks and bonds in producing companies.

Compounding of interest: The most powerful tool at an investor's disposal. Allows investors to earn interest on their interest.

Consumer confidence: Tells us how people feel about spending. If they are confident, people spend more. Spending drives the economy up. People cut spending if they are concerned about the economy.

Consumer price index (CPI): A basket of goods and services tracked by the Bureau of Labor Statistics that measure the relative price change from month to month. This change is the rate of inflation.

Convertible bond: Corporate bond that can be converted into stock if you think the company will do well in the future.

Corporate bond: Most risky of all bonds. Issued based on the financial strength of the company – can be risky if issued from a company in poor financial health. Denominations of $1,000.

Coupon rate: See "Fixed interest rate."

Currency trading: The largest market in the world.

Cyclical stock: Tends to move with the economy. Grows or slows as the economy grows or slows. (Example: Commodity stocks.)

D

Day order: An order to buy or sell a stock that is canceled at the close of trading the day the order is placed.

Day's range: A stock's highest price and lowest price for that trading day.

Day trader: Make or lose money by small swings in price on a large number of shares in one trading session.

Default: The bond issuer can't pay interest or return all of face value.

Depression: Marks a decline of 10% or more in the GDP along with a recession lasting more than two years.

Derivative: Security that's based on other investment products.

Discount/online broker: Takes an investing order from a buyer or seller over the phone or online.

Discount/online-with-assistance broker: A broker that provides more assistance to the buyer and seller (like additional research or newsletters with investing tips), but will not necessarily offer stock recommendations.

Discretionary account: Gives the broker the right to buy and sell stock without notifying you.

Diversification: Spreading your investment money between different stocks and sectors so you don't put all your eggs in one basket.

Dividend: A payment of profits to the owner of a stock. Board of Directors sets dividend rate.

Dividend investing: See "Income investing."

Dividend reinvestment plan (DRIP): Automatically reinvests the dividends you earn from a stock to buy more shares and earn you even more dividends.

Dividend yield: Percent representation of how much a company pays to its shareholders per year in dividends based on the current share price.

Dow Jones Industrial Average: Oldest and most widely known stock index – contains 30 stocks.

Durable goods: Items that last more than three years. Cars and major appliances are durable goods.

E

Earnings: The profit a company creates. This is the single most important number when evaluating a company.

Earnings per share (EPS): Valuation ratio that measures a company's profitability and is important in determining a reasonable share price at which to invest. The higher the EPS, the more profitable the company.

Economic indicators: Key measures of the economy's health, such as unemployment, wages, and prices.

Economic moat: One or more big advantages a great company has over its competitors that help it continue to be a great investment.

Electronic communication networks (ECN): Connect buyers and sellers directly without going through an exchange.

Exchange-traded funds (ETFs): Funds that are similar to mutual funds but are traded on the open market like stocks. Many ETFs follow narrow indexes such as the S&P 500. Others focus on a particular industry segment.

Exercise: To put into effect the right specified in the contract. For instance, the option buyer can "exercise" his right to buy shares at the strike price.

Exit strategy: A plan for how and when to sell a stock.

Expiration date: The date when the option ends or expires. Option contracts generally expire on the third Friday of each month.

F

Face value: ["Stated principal."] The stated principal on a loan – what a bondholder pays when a bond is issued and what he gets back at maturity.

Federal Reserve Board (the "Fed"): Controls the nation's interest rates by setting the key interest rates charged to banks.

Fitch – AAA rating: The best-quality companies – reliable and stable.

Fitch – AA rating: Quality companies – a bit higher risk than AAA.

Fitch – A rating: Economic situation can affect finances.

Fitch – BBB rating: Medium-class companies, which are satisfactory at that moment.

Fitch – BB, B rating: More prone to changes in the economy.

Fixed interest rate: ["Coupon rate", "Nominal yield"] Rate of interest a bond pays until maturity.

Fixed maturity: The defined life of a bond.

Foreign fund: ["Global fund"] Mutual fund that invests in foreign stocks and bonds focusing on a particular area of the global economy.

Forex (FX): Foreign exchange market for trading currencies, mostly for speculations from hedge funds, large institutional investors, and individuals.

Forex quote: Always the first currency compared to the second (example: "EUR/USD"). Noted to four decimal points.

Full-service broker: A stockbroker that provides specific stock recommendations. Conducts a financial assessment to determine your needs and suitability for various investments. And puts together an investing plan.

G

General obligation bond: Municipal bond that pays a slightly higher interest rate than Treasury issues. Rated on the creditworthiness of the issuer. Proceeds are used to build roads, utilities, and other improvements.

Good 'til canceled order: An order to buy or sell a stock at a set price that remains active until you cancel it or until the trade is executed.

Gross domestic product (GDP): A measure of the total value of goods and services produced. Results issued quarterly and are considered a gauge of the economy's health.

Growth fund: Mutual fund that invests in high-growth companies and sectors for much higher returns than the broad market.

Growth investing: A strategy where investors look for great companies that are growing rapidly… and have the potential to keep growing.

Growth stock: Grows rapidly in price as the company grows. As the company's growth slows over time, the stock's growth also slows.

H

Hard stop loss: Set price at which you decide to sell your investment to protect against a falling market. Designed to minimize your losses.

I

Income investing: ["Dividend investing"] A strategy where investors are more interested in current and future income than capital gains through share-price growth.

Income statement: Part of the financial statement that reports revenue (sales) and expenses. Indicates if the company is making a profit or not.

Income stock: Pays a consistent and growing dividend.

Index: Tracks the activity of a selected group of stocks, bonds, or other securities over time.

Index fund: Mutual fund that tracks various stock and bond indexes.

Interest rate: The Federal Reserve Board (the Fed) sets interest rates. Its actions affect both what you pay for a loan and what you receive for a savings investment.

Initial margin: Small cash outlay to buy a futures contract (less than the total value of a contract).

Initial public offering (IPO): When a company goes public and begins selling shares of stock in the market.

Intrinsic value: The true value of a company as measured by variables beyond the financial statements.

Investing: An active way to increase your net worth.

Investor: Buys stocks based on the value of the business and whether it will grow over a long period.

K

Key economic report: Government report issued on important indicators about the health of the economy. Investors should know what these indicators mean.

L

Large-cap stock: A company with a market capitalization of $10 billion-$200 billion.

Leverage: The use of borrowed money to increase your return.

Leveraged fund: Mutual fund that borrows money to increase potential returns. Track certain stock indexes.

Liabilities: What a company owes to others.

Limit order: Instructs your broker to buy or sell a stock at a particular price. Order won't be filled until the stock reaches your specified price.

Load: A fee paid to salespeople. Commission for broker who sold mutual fund.

M

Margin account: Allows you to borrow up to 50% of the value of the stock from your broker. This allows you to potentially multiply your profits dramatically. Risky for beginning investors.

Market capitalization: Measures the total market value of a company's stock. Market cap = outstanding shares x price of one share.

Market order: Instructs your broker to buy or sell stock immediately for the current market price. Simplest and quickest way to get your order filled.

Market price: The price of the last trade made on a stock. Shows up at the current price on services like Yahoo Finance and Google Finance.

Mega-cap stock: A company with a market capitalization of more than $200 billion.

Micro-cap stock: A company with a market capitalization of less than $300 million.

Mid-cap stock: A company with a market capitalization of $2 billion-$10 billion.

Money manager: A stockbroker that handles large portfolios. Takes responsibility for investment decisions in exchange for a percentage of the assets managed.

Money market fund: Mutual fund that invests in cash-equivalent securities such as short-term U.S. Treasury bills.

Moody's – Aaa rating: Highest-quality bond with the smallest degree of risk. Interest payments are protected by an exceptionally stable margin and principal is secure.

Moody's – Aa, A rating: High-quality bond by all standards. Margins of protection may not be as large as in Aaa securities.

Moody's – Baa rating: These bonds possess many favorable investment attributes. Factors giving security to principal and interest are considered adequate.

Moody's – Ba, B rating: Bond lacks outstanding investment characteristics and has speculative characteristics.

Municipal bond (muni): Bonds issued by governmental units such as states, counties, and cities. Often exempt from federal income tax.

Mutual fund: A way for investors to pool their money into a particular group of investments – stocks, bonds, combinations, and money market funds.

N

Nasdaq: One of two major U.S. stock exchanges. First all-electronic exchange. Home of the technology industry.

Nasdaq Composite Index: Covers the almost 3,000 stocks and other securities traded on the Nasdaq exchange.

Net asset value (NAV): The mutual-fund equivalent of a share price. This is the price you buy and sell mutual fund shares at if you deal directly with the company.

New factory orders: Rise or fall in factory orders indicates the rate of economic growth. More new factory orders suggests the economy is growing.

New York Stock Exchange (NYSE): One of two major U.S. stock exchanges. Constitution was drafted in 1817. Home to the oldest and most prestigious companies in America.

Nominal yield: See "Fixed interest rate."

Non-cyclical stock: Does not react much to economic moves. (Example: Consumer staples.)

O

Open-end mutual fund: Issues new shares when someone wants to buy into the fund. Buys them back when the investor wants to sell.

Opening price: Price point where a stock begins trading for that day.

Option: Gives the owner the right, but not the obligation, to buy or sell a certain number of shares of stock at a fixed price on or before a certain date.

Options agreement: Spells out what the limitations of buying options are and lists your responsibilities.

Over the Counter (OTC): A way to trade stocks that are too small for listing on one of the major exchanges.

P

Passively managed mutual fund: Tracks specific stocks or market indexes, such as the S&P 500 or the Dow. The fund mirrors the index by investing in the stocks that comprise the index.

Precious metal fund: Mutual fund that focuses on precious metals such as gold and silver.

Preferred shares: A type of security with a higher claim on the assets and earnings of a company than common stock. Preferred shareholders get paid their dividend before common shareholders.

Premium: The price an option buyer pays. It is quoted on a per-share basis. Options are traded in 100-share lots, so you pay 100 times the quoted premium.

Previous close: The price of the last trade for a stock the previous day.

Price: What a stock trades for at any point in time.

Price-to-book (P/B) ratio: Tells you how much a company is worth and if that value is reflected in the stock price.

Price-to-earnings (P/E) ratio: Valuation metric that gives you an idea of what the market is willing to pay for the company's earnings. The higher the P/E, the more the market is willing to pay. Most popular metric of stock analysis.

Price-to-earnings-growth (PEG) ratio: The P/E ratio divided by the projected growth rate of earnings.

Price-to-sales (P/S) ratio: Compares companies in any sector with each other. Provides a way to look at young companies with no earnings.

Prospectus: The formal document a company must file with the Securities & Exchange Commission (SEC) as a request to "go public" – sell shares of its stock on the open market. The document must contain facts that an investor needs to make an informed investment decision.

Put-option buyer: Has the right, but not the obligation, to sell the stock at a certain price by a certain date.

Put-option seller: Has the obligation to buy the stock at a certain price by a certain date.

R

Real estate investment trust (REIT): A special security that invests in real estate projects either directly or by buying mortgages.

Recession: A decline in the nation's gross domestic product for two consecutive quarters.

Return on equity (ROE): Measure of how efficiently a company uses its assets to produce earnings.

Revenue bond: Municipal bond used to build projects that will create a revenue stream – like toll roads. Riskier than general-obligation bond because the revenue bond is not backed by a taxing authority.

Reverse stock split: Share split that reduces the number of shares outstanding. In a "1 for 2" split, 50 million shares become 25 million shares. The market doubles the price of the stock.

S

S&P 500 Index: Most widely used proxy of the market – 500 largest publicly traded corporations.

S&P – AAA rating: The bond issuer's capacity to meet its financial obligation is extremely strong.

S&P – AA, A rating: The bond issuer's capacity to meet its financial obligation is very strong.

S&P – BBB, BBB rating: These bonds are somewhat suscep-tible to the adverse effects of changing economic conditions. But the bond issuer's capacity to meet its financial obliga-tions is strong.

S&P – BB+, BB, B rating: Adverse economic conditions are more likely to lead to a weakened capacity of the bond issuer to meet its financial commitment.

Saving: A passive form of money management through sav-ings accounts, bank CDs, and short-term U.S. Treasury prod-ucts (like T-bills).

Sector ETF: Lets you zero in on a part of the stock market that you believe is moving in one direction or the other.

Sector fund: Mutual fund that invests in narrow sectors of the stock and bond markets.

Securities and Exchange Commission (SEC): Regulates the stock market.

Shareholders' equity: Liabilities subtracted from assets.

Small-cap stock: A company with a market capitalization of $300 million-$2 billion.

Spread: The difference between the bid and ask price.

Stated principal: See "Face value."

Statement of cash flow: Tracks cash from operating, financial, and investing operations. Picture of how a company manages operations and helps overcome accounting adjustments to the income statement.

Stockbroker: Facilitates trades for the buyer or seller.

Stock buyback: The company buys its own shares to increase its per-share price. Reduced supply of shares creates higher demand for remaining shares.

Stock fund: Mutual fund that invests primarily in common stock.

Stock index: A basket of stocks that represents all or certain segments of the market. Most investors consider the S&P 500 Index representative of the market, while the Dow is still the best-known.

Stock price: Amount a buyer and seller agree on. May change for every trade.

Stock quote: What the security is currently trading for.

Stock screens: Services like MorningStar or Yahoo Finance that allow you to set parameters and search for only those stocks that match your investment requirements.

Stock sectors: Groupings of common industry types.

Stock split: A company splits its existing shares into more shares. In a "2 for 1" split, 50 million shares become 100 million shares. The market reduces the price of the stock by half.

Stock symbol: Abbreviations of a company name that make it easier to search for on finance websites.

Stop-loss order: Gives your broker a price trigger that protects you from a big drop in a stock.

Strike price: The price at which the option can be exercised. It is part of the option quote.

T

Traders: Buy and sell stocks on short-term swings in prices. Riskier than investing.

Trailing stop loss: A stop loss designed to maximize your gains. It's set a certain percentage below a stock's current market price. And it rises as the share price rises.

Treasury bill: Safest of all investment choices. Maturity of four to 26 weeks – should be classified as "cash management." Sold at a discount to face value. You receive the face value at maturity. Difference is your interest earned.

Treasury bond: Maturity of 10-plus years. Denominations of $1,000 up to $1 million. Popular with large institutional investors. Pays interest every six months.

Treasury inflation protected securities (TIPS): Bonds with maturities of five, 10, and 20 years. Auctioned in denominations of $1,000. Adjusted for inflation.

Treasury note: Two-, three-, five-, or 10-year maturities. Denominations of $1,000. Interest rate is set when sold at auction. Notes with 10-year maturities are tied to the 30-year home-mortgage rate.

U

Unemployment (jobs): Important economic indicator showing the number of employed people. High unemployment means consumers are not spending money at a rate that boosts the economy.

U.S. Treasury issues: Backed by the "full faith and credit" of the U.S. government. Very safe, low return. Exempt from state and local taxes.

V

Value: What a company is worth as an ongoing business.

Value fund: Mutual fund that invests in securities the market hasn't priced correctly.

Value investing: Investing in stocks that are worth more – according to earnings growth, dividends, cash flow, and book value – than the current market price.

Value stock: A company that's trading below its true value.

Volume: Number of shares traded in a period – sometimes reported in millions.

Y

Yield: Another way to say "return." Expressed as a percentage.

More from Stansberry Research

The World's Greatest Investment Ideas

The Stansberry Research Trader's Manual

The Doctor's Protocol Field Manual

High Income Retirement:
How to Safely Earn 12% to 20%
Income Streams on Your Savings

World Dominating Dividend Growers:
Income Streams That Never Go Down

Secrets of the Natural Resource Market:
How to Set Yourself up for Huge Returns
in Mining, Energy, and Agriculture

The Stansberry Research Starter's Guide for New Investors

The Living Cure:
The Promise of Cancer Immunotherapy

97458773R00099

Made in the USA
Middletown, DE
05 November 2018